MENTORING AMONG AFRICAN AMERICAN WOMEN

Attitudes and Preferences

By

Dr. Tiffany Manning

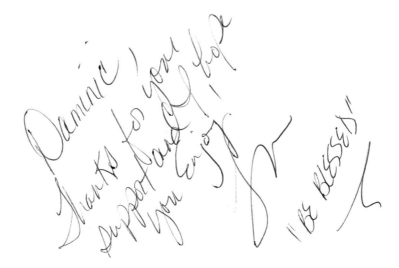

Table of Contents

List of Tables

4

"Give light and people will find the way." – *Ella Josephine Baker*

CHAPTER 1. INTRODUCTION

Introduction to the Problem

Mentoring is a tool used for many years that has focused on assisting less experienced individuals with becoming more experienced. In recent years, studies have oftentimes examined the concept of mentoring from the protégé point of view (Allen, 2007). It is imperative, however, to understand the concept of mentoring from the perspectives of the protégé and of the mentor. The process of mentoring involves the mentor and protégé working in partnership within well-defined roles and responsibilities to enhance the mentorship experience. Successful mentoring relationships have played a significant role in career advancement and job satisfaction (Strauss, Johnson, Mallory, Marquez, & Feldman, 2013; Allen).

Any deficiency or lack of effort in delivering the agreed upon outcome of the relationship, on behalf of the mentor, could potentially leave a gap in clearly defining the mentorship process and what works during mentoring. The failure to provide specific causes why the mentoring relationship did not work will lessen theoretical development in the field (Strauss et al., 2013; Allen, 2007). Mentors are a significant element to the continuous success of organizations. Kram and Hall (1996) posited that mentors possess the ability to transfer valid organization knowledge to entry level co-workers that clearly defines those individuals organizational responsibility. Dedicated and appropriate mentors are instrumental in the success of formal mentoring programs with organizations (Allen, Eby, & Lentz, 2006; Allen & Poteet, 1999; Ragins, Cotton, & Miller, 2000). Organizations sometimes use matching systems to ensure that the appropriate mentor is paired with a suitable protégé. It is important, however, for the protégé to be able to identify with their mentor. Matching systems comprise identifying matching skills, personalities, and characteristics to which the protégé and mentor would work

6

best together (Ragins, Cotton, & Miller).

Noe (1988) suggested that inadequate access to informal networks and mentors explains the differences in career advancement of men and women. Kram (1985), on the other hand, stated that a small number of female role models are to be blamed since women seem to be more passive in assuming mentoring responsibilities. Women are perceived to be more reluctant to become mentors due to barriers such as time constraints, token status, and lack of self-confidence (Kram). In today's society, women can be often intimidated by other women (Bell & Nkomo, 2001). This level of intimidation could be a reason for their hesitancy to mentor other women. Additionally, time constraints could also be an added factor as to why women (preferably single mothers) find it hard to engage in mentoring relationships since they usually bear the roles of full-time employee and parent.

Women, like men, are just as suitable to become mentors. Allen, Poteet, Russell, and Dobbins (1997) identified organizational level as a factor that affects their willingness to mentor others. The scholarly study of workplace mentoring within the field of Human Service leadership is an area that has not received an extensive amount of empirical attention. Ragin and Cotton (1993) examined workplace mentoring in their study on gender and willingness to mentor in organizations. Their study focused on mentor attitude versus mentor gender by examining the attitudes in mentoring among male and female. This study, conversely, will examine the attitudes of the female gender in mentoring.

Women have advanced in organizations becoming leaders in an attempt at becoming equal to their counterparts. Women now hold the same positions as men and, in some circumstances, earn the same salary. Nevertheless, these improvements may not pertain to the career advancement of African American women in leadership positions (Combs, 2003).

7

African American women still face convergence of race and gender relative to career advancement and improving their organizational standing (Combs). Race and gender appears to be holding African American women back in the leadership sector of Human Services. According to Combs African American women may be less available and may operate under different terms than that of African American men, white women, and men who hold leadership positions. Thorough examination of the impact of race and gender on informal networks (like that of a mentoring relationship) of African American women in human services leadership positions seems well-needed and appropriate. This study will examine mentoring among African American women in Human Service leadership positions.

Background of the Study

Leadership is an important component that affects organizational performance. Packard (2004) affirmed that it contributes to an organization's culture, climate, and performance. While research on leadership in Human Service organizations has increased, there is still a limited amount of research knowledge to guide practice in the field. The improvement of Human Service organizational climate and culture, in reference to leadership development, is important. Leaders in the field of Human Services are confronted with various individuals' social and economic challenges (Human Services Summit, 2010). Therefore, it is imperative for them to be properly prepared to face these challenges and develop effective leadership qualities that would motivate their passion to participate in mentoring relationships. Moreover, making mentoring opportunities more readily available will allow for future leaders to be more accessible. It will also aid in changing the face of leadership and provide the opportunity for followers to become more identifiable with their leaders.

The Human Services Value Curve involves four different models - Regulative Business Model, Collaborative Business Model, Integrative Business Model, and Generative Business Model. Within the Generative Business Model, the Human Services organization focuses on addressing multi-dimensional family problems, socioeconomic issues, and opportunities required to generate community and individual success (Human Services Summit, 2010). At that level, social networks help synthesize information and trends across ecosystems within organizations. The Generative Business Model utilizes evidence-based practices to ascertain and substantiate that mentoring relationships are an important part of organizational success (Human Services Summit).

When using a Generative Business Model, the selection or pairing process used to connect mentors and protégés is critical. Furthermore, protégé willingness to learn is an essential requirement of protégé selection (Allen, 2003). Allen indicated that, in the selection process, mentor aspirations or motives for mentoring varies when considering the importance of protégé ability and willingness to learn. Allen also suggested that mentors who are motivated by the want to enhance themselves are more likely to indicate that protégé ability is more important in the protégé selection process. On the other hand, mentors motivated by intrinsic satisfaction are more likely to favor protégé willingness to learn as important in the protégé selection process.

According to the United States Census Bureau (2007), women make up 51% the United States population. Of this 51% of the population, 46% of these women are in the workforce. However, women are noticeably missing in senior level leadership positions (Billett, 2003). Though women, as an overall population, are underrepresented in upper level positions, studies show that Caucasian women are outpacing African American women in upper level positions and pay that have been traditionally reserved for the Caucasian and African American male

9

populations (King & Gomez, 2007). It appears then that African American women are being outpaced in upper level positions due to gender and race.

Although African American women are thriving in Human Services, they still hold very few leadership positions. There is no study to date examining the attitudes and preferences of African American women in mentoring within Human Services leadership. This study will focus on the preferences of African American women as they relate to components of protégé selection. African American women will be selected for this study because of the limited number of them involved in mentoring relationships within Human Services (Billett, 2003). If there were more African American women in leadership roles within Human Services, there would be more opportunities for them to mentor. This study will contribute to current mentoring literature by offering information from the perspective of a female mentor within Human Services leadership.

It is important for African American women to be able to examine literature which will contribute to their understanding of what components are important when mentoring African American female protégés. Bell (1990) asserted that mentoring is valuable because of its interpersonal function. Additionally, mentoring teaches African American women to embrace their unique bi-cultural identity as a tool of empowerment instead of distress (Bell).

Statement of the Problem

Catalyst (2004), is a study that examined African American women in the workforce, it affirmed that African American women are a growing source of talent in the corporate sector that are faced with several challenges when mentoring in the Human Services field. These challenges include, but are not limited to, availability of mentoring opportunities and interference with professional development. The mentoring literature lacks sufficient research that clearly identifies the vast number of challenges that these women face. There is an abundance of mentoring literature currently available, but most of the mentoring literature examines the mentoring relationship from the protégé's perspective (Allen, 2007; Allen & Poteet, 1999; Ragins, Cotton, & Miller, 2000).

This study will examine the mentoring relationship from the mentor's perspective. Young and Perrewe (2000) discovered that mentors are more satisfied with mentoring relationships that involve a protégé who is open to advisement and coaching. No qualitative study to date has directly examined a protégé's willingness to learn as a factor in the selection process by mentors (Allen, 2004). This study will examine, from the viewpoint of an African American female mentor, the perspectives of a protégé's willingness to learn as a factor in the selection process.

Purpose of the Study

The current study will contribute to the mentoring research by examining the attitudes and preferences in mentoring of African American women. This study's investigation will be guided by the empirical works of Ragins and Scandura (1999) and Allen, Poteet, and Russell (2000). Ragins and Scandura and Allen et al. shed light on the protégé selection process and career advancement from the view of the protégé. The purpose of this study is to bridge the gap in mentoring literature and to further the previous research by providing an understanding of the protégé selection process and the potential for career advancement from the view of the mentor.

Rationale of the Study

In the Human Services sector, African American women have climbed to the senior level leadership positions over the past several decades at a slow and stagnant pace. African American women make up 46.7% of the Human Services sector of the labor force in America (Catalyst, 2009). Of this 46.7%, less than half occupy senior level positions. While this statistic shows an increase in the number of African American women in senior level positions, the research also suggests that the rate of this increase has been minimal. This low rate of increase is due to the lack of opportunities given to African American women (Straus, Johnson, Marquez, & Feldman, 2013). In order for more mentoring opportunities to be afforded to women of color, there needs to be more opportunities for leadership positions. A lack of leadership opportunities could potentially result in a lack of mentoring opportunities. Hence, African American women mentors could become inaccessible.

Mentoring is a key component that assists senior level executives to influence entry- level employees to realize, reach for, and maximize their potential (Allen et al., 2006). Mentoring literature on African American women in Human Service leadership is minimal. Ragins and Scandura (1999) examined mentoring relationship from the view of the protégé. A gap, however, exists in the literature concerning mentoring relationships from the perspective of the mentor. An understanding of the perspective of mentoring relationships in African American women from the mentor's perspective could add to the knowledge-base concerning mentoring relationships. This study examined the perspective of the mentor and explored new avenues by focusing on African American women in Human Service leadership positions.

Research Questions

The mentoring relationship is a key component when considering career advancement and career satisfaction (Straus et al., 2013). This study examined the attitudes and preferences in mentoring among African American women in Human Service leadership. The study was guided by the following research questions:

RQ1: How do African American women mentors in Human Service leadership select their protégés?

RQ2: What are the attitudes of African American women in Human Service leadership regarding the effect of mentoring on their career advancement?

Significance of the Study

The ability and availability to advance in a career are very important career components. Mentoring relationships are influential with assisting entry level employees in advancing to senior level positions (Straus et al., 2013). While many African American women hold senior level positions in Human Services, the literature presents limited knowledge concerning on mentoring relationships among African American women in Human Service leadership. This study will, therefore, seek to provide information regarding the significance of mentoring relationships among African American women and add to the knowledge base concerning mentoring relationships.

The racial identity development of African American women accompanied with the changing bi-cultural workforce could potentially have an influence on their attitudes and preferences. Without the proper coaching or training of more experienced African American women, entry level employees may lose the desire to advance in their career, or may lose the desire to assist others in advancing in their career. It is, however, imperative that opportunities are offered for African American women to provide expertise on how to advance at work and in life to other African American women (Crawford & Smith, 2005). African American women can identify with other African American women in ways that individuals from other races are not able to identify. Identification of relevant and applicable dynamics relative to mentoring relationships among African American women allows organizations to strengthen those dynamics that could provide mentoring opportunities for these women. The significance of the discovery relative to mentoring relationships could help bridge the gap in mentoring literature and further the research by providing an understanding of the protégé selection process from the view of the mentor.

Definition of Terms

Bicultural. Staying grounded with your African American identity and culture while balancing a career and professional identity in the Caucasian culture (Bell, 1990).

Collaborative Business Model. A business model that includes Regulative, Collaborative, Integrative, and Generative features that are aimed at achieving desired and sustainable outcomes. A collaborative business model also aims at empowering the workforce (APHSA, 2013).

Generative Business Model. The level of focus where a Human Services organization addresses multi-dimensional family problems and socioeconomic issues that assist with generating long-term community and individual success (APHSA, 2013).

Human Service. Human Services focuses on achieving a humans needs through an interdisciplinary knowledge base.

Integrative Business Model. The level of focus in a Human Services organization where the goal is to complete integration of multiple programs and services in order to improve services for the client, increase participation, and support data driven policy and decision making (APHSA, 2013).

Leader-Member Exchange (LMX) Theory. LMX theory is a transactional approach of how supervisors use their power and organizational resources for the development of exchange relationships with different subordinates (Scandura & Schriesheim, 1994).

Mentor. A more experienced person who gives advice and training to a less experienced individual (Merriam-Webster, 2014).

Protégé. A less experienced person who receives guidance from a more experienced person (Merriam-Webster, 2014).

Racial Identity. A sense of group or collective identity based on an individual belief one has of their common heritage with a particular racial group (Thompson & Carter, 1997).

Value Curve. The Human Services Value Curve was created to transform an organization's business model from ineffective to one that focuses on generating effective individuals and communities by co-creating effective solutions for multi-dimensional socioeconomic challenges (APHSA, 2013).

Assumptions

This generic qualitative study examined the attitudes and preferences from the perspective of the mentor by focusing on African American women in Human Service leadership positions. A number of assumptions are conditional to the study. The first assumption is that the participants of the study will be open to the interview process and to honestly share their experiences. Given that confidentiality and anonymity will be guaranteed for the study, the second assumption is that the responses to the interview questions by the research participants will be sincere and honest and that the information they provide will be appropriate to share. The final assumption is that the perspectives of the mentors will contribute data that will add practical and valuable information to the field of Human Services and to African American women leadership positions.

Limitations

This study will not be without some limitations. First, the study will focus only on Human Service organizations. As a result, the findings will not be generalized to all other organizations that will not be studied (Mertens, 2005; Nardi, 2003). Second, the study will be limited by the perspectives of certain individuals who willingly choose to participate in the study. The research, therefore, will not be generalizable to all African American women in Human Service leadership positions. In addition, the experiences of the research participants will not be expressive of the experiences of all African American women in Human Service leadership positions in twenty-first century organizations. Lastly, the study will also be limited by the ability to discover themes and realize the true meaning of the experiences of the research participants.

Conceptual Framework

The purpose of this study is to examine attitudes and preferences among African American women mentors. Mentoring is defined as a relationship between a less experienced individual (the mentee or protégé) and an individual with more experience (the mentor) (Davis,

2001). The study will further seek to examine the attitudes of African American women relative to the effect of mentoring on career advancement and the reward or fulfillment achieved from mentoring. The research will also explore mentors preferences concerning protégé selection and protégé specific qualities. A generic qualitative research approach will be utilized for this study in order to obtain the true meaning of the experiences and perspections of attitudes and preferences among African American women mentors and the effect of mentoring on career advancement.

The mentoring relationship involves a series of exchanges between the mentor and protégé. The exchange comprises information sharing among each other and in return, the protégé acquires leadership guidance from the mentor. In view of these relationship exchanges, the study will also utilize an LMX theory approach to give authority to the experiences of the mentors. An LMX approach is identified as having a persuasive influence on how effective and worthwhile the leader-follower relationship could become (Whitener et al., 1998) and how supervisors use their power and organizational resources for the development of exchange relationships with different subordinates (Scandura & Schriesheim, 1994). Taking into consideration that the experiences of African American women mentors are legitimate by using an LMX approach, it seems adequate to consider that an understanding of the experiences of African American women relative to mentoring (the relationship shared between the mentor and protégé), the effect of mentoring on career advancement, and the fulfillment experienced from mentoring could be attained by exploring the lived experiences of mentors who have experienced mentoring relationships in Human Services organizations.

Organization of the Remainder of the Study

Chapter 1 presented the problem statement, purpose of the study, significance of the study of the research, and identified the research questions. Chapter 2 will present a review of the literature to support the study. Included in Chapter 2 will be an in-depth exploration of mentoring and the development of mentoring relationships as they relate to race, gender, and previous mentoring experiences, mentoring in the workplace, social exchange theory, and racial identity development. Chapter 2 will also examine the origins of Leader-Member Exchange Theory and Racial Identity Development Theory. There will also be an examination of Leader Skills Competencies and Mentoring Based Practices. Chapter 3 will expound on the research methodology that will be utilized for the study. The data collection and synopsis of the results will be presented in Chapter 4. Lastly, Chapter 5 will present a discussion of the research results and will comprise the study's conclusions, limitations, and recommendations for future research.

CHAPTER 2. LITERATURE REVIEW

Introduction

The interest in workplace developmental relationships has increased since it was discovered that these relationships play a vital role in career progression and success (Eby, Rhodes, & Allen, 2007). Mentoring has become important in organizational development (Eby et al.) due to its contribution to career advancement, positive self-growth, and awareness (Dubois, Holloway, Valentine, & Cooper, 2002; Eby et al; Kram, 1985). The focus of this literature review is on mentoring and the development of mentoring relationships relative to race, gender, previous mentoring experiences, mentoring in the workplace, leader-member exchange theory, and racial identity development. Additionally, the empirical works of Ragins and Cotton (1993) and Combs (2003) will be discussed. This literature review will also discuss how mentoring and leadership have an impact on organizational success.

Mentoring

The ideas and definitions surrounding mentoring can be traced back to Greek mythology in the story of Odysseus (Hansman, 2002). Odysseus asked his female friend to assume a male role as a mentor while he was away at battle (Hansman). Thus, the name mentor was used to describe people who were beneficial to others and described them as helpful teachers. This idea of mentor has continued through centuries and is reflected in the vast number of definitions associated with mentoring (Hansman). The one commonality that all definitions of mentoring have in common is that the relationship involves a mentor and protégé – a more experienced individual passing on knowledge to a less experienced individual.

Reflections of past definitions of mentoring can also be found in the expectations

19

associated with mentoring relationships (Colvin, 2010). A mentor is referred to as a teacher, advisor, or sponsor (Levinson, Darrow, Klein, & Levinson, 1978). This allows the meaning of mentoring to be open to personal or professional reference. For this study, the definition of mentoring is associated with helping with professional life (Ragins, 1997). Ragins described mentoring as people with advanced experience and knowledge who are willing to provide insight or support to those with less experience.

Research regarding perceived barriers to mentoring has been mixed. Ragins and Cotton (1993) discovered that women perceived greater barriers to mentoring than men. They further affirmed the existence of gender differences in the willingness to mentor others. In contrast, Allen, Poteet, Russell, and Dobbins (1997) posited no differences in reference to gender and Ragins and Scandura (1994) found no differences between executive-level men and women. Ragins and Scandura concluded that gender differences in willingness to mentor others may be a function of gender differences in rank, position, and resources.

Gender Differences

Canary and Dindia (1998) posited that males and females tend to respond differently to helping relationships with women placing a higher value on interpersonal support than men. Studies examining gender differences in outcomes among program participants have been widespread and inconclusive (DuBois, Holloway, Valentine, & Cooper; Rhodes, Lowe, Litchfield, & Walsh-Samp, 2002). None of these studies have looked at the differences in relationship quality and/or how long the relationship last (Rhodes, Lowe, Litchfield, & Walsh-Samp). Consequently, findings regarding gender specific approaches in mentoring remain unanswered.

Eagly and Crowley (1986) found that men offered and responded to more instrumental forms of helping while women offered more social, nurturing and caring forms of support. In particular, Ragins and Sundstrom (1989) suggested that because females have less power, face sexism, and are perceived as more vulnerable than men and their relationships with mentors serve more psychosocial roles. Ragins (1999) argued that gender needs to be considered in workplace mentoring for it to be successful. These findings proceeded Ragins & Cotton (1993) study which posited that the female mentor to female protégé scenario lessens complications related to cross-gender mentoring and suggested it is the most visible of all gender combinations.

Previously the female mentor to female protégé scenario was met with negative reactions because it was viewed as constituting a female power coalition (Ragins & Cotton, 1993). Today same sex mentoring relationships are encouraged because of their impact on individual and organizational success (Davidson & Foster-Johnson, 2001). Women will be able to identify with other women on a more personal and professional level. In essence, same gender mentoring relationships for females will allow for psychosocial support to be reciprocated. The current study examined same sex mentoring relationships among African American women in Human Service leadership.

Mentoring and Career Development

Ragins and Cotton (1993) discovered that women perceived greater barriers to mentoring than men. However, they found no support for the hypothesis that willingness to mentor others would be related to age. The current study examined willingness to mentor others as it relates to race and gender, rather than age. Mentoring relationships have proven to be beneficial for mentors and protégés of all ages, races, and gender (Ragins & Cotton; Kram, 1985).

Kram (1985) suggested that mentors should assist in providing career functions and

21

psychosocial support. These functions are provided over time and may vary in the way they are administered. There is empirical evidence that protégés experience desirable work and career outcomes as a result of workplace mentoring (Ragins & Verbos, 2007). Mentors may sometimes develop the passion to mentor because of their past experience as a protégé.

The relationship is beneficial to protégés as it relates to career advancement, career development, and career satisfaction (Ragins & Cotton, 1993; Scandura, 1992). Kram (1985) affirmed that the mentor views the relationship as an important career developmental component. While the mentoring relationship is important for the mentor and protégé, the intrinsic force surrounding the individual motivation to participate is different (Ragins & Cotton). According to Ragin and Cotton (1993), mentoring has become a huge part of the managerial/leadership role within organizations. Managers and leaders are expected to provide career assistance to entry-level employees (protégés) (Ragins & Cotton; Feldman, 1988; Hall, 1987). Leaders of organizations have the responsibility to ensure that the company experiences continued success and to ensure that entry-level employees receive necessary guidance and training that propels organizational success (Ragins & Cotton). Mentoring allows mangers and leaders (male or female) to offer less experienced employees (male or female) an opportunity to train for future leadership roles.

While mentoring is important for both men and women, Solomon, Bishop, and Bresser (1986) proposed that mentoring is critical for women in organizations. They also insinuated that it is important for female protégés to have access to female mentors because these mentors can provide essential role modeling functions. Female mentor to female protégé can help alleviate sexual issues common to female protégé to male mentor relationships (Ragins & Cotton, 1993; Clawson & Kram, 1984). Women are, therefore, encouraged to seek out a mentor or become one

22

(Ragins & Cotton). Previous theories on the development of mentoring relationships indicated women face gender related barriers to becoming a mentor (Kram, 1985).

According to Kanter (1977), women in management face more obstacles in mentoring than their male counterparts because women are a numerical minority. Because of this numerical rarity, female mentors are more visible (Ragins & Cotton, 1993). When things happen that are of the norm, they can sometimes go without notice (Ragins & Cotton). However, when rare instances occur, it is usually more visible and stands out. This is one risk that was discovered that is directly associated with same sex mentoring, as it relates to protégé performance (Ragins & Cotton, 1993). Protégé performance is often viewed as a reflection of the mentor's competency and being a mentor to a low performing protégé is a risk that some female mentors may not be willing to take in their careers (Ragins & Cotton).

Workforce Diversity

As previously discussed, Ragins and Cotton's (1993) study results indicated that same sex mentoring relationships are an important component in the dynamic of mentoring. However, their study did not offer information on how race and gender will affect the mentoring dynamic. Understanding the interactive effect of race and gender is critical in identifying the position and quality of the participation of managerial African American women in the workplace (Combs, 2003).

Acquiring knowledge of and across different racial groups is critical considering the diversity of organizations and the composition of the people within those organizations (Murrell & Hayes-James, 2001). These diverse interactions will definitely involve intersections of race and mentoring. There are several trends and themes that underscore the need to more fully explore the intersection of race and mentoring such as workforce diversity.

23

While diversity in workforce participation is increasing, it is not at every level of the organization. According to Catalyst (2001), the number of women of color in the workforce has increased, but they still only represent 1.1% of corporate officers in Fortune 500 firms. Their research outlines some of the barriers that are faced, particularly by women of color who often have a "double disadvantage" within traditional organizations (Bell, 1990; Murrell, 1999). Some of the barriers identified include: minimal opportunities for promotion, minimal opportunities for same-race mentoring networks, and minimal opportunities for same-gender mentoring networks (Bell).

Informal and Formal Networks

The multi-definitions of mentoring are used to describe informal and formal mentoring relationships. Kram and Isabella (1985) defined informal mentoring relationships as relationships that are psychosocial and enhance protégé self-esteem. Informal mentoring relationships help build confidence through interpersonal connections, emotional stability, and mutual discovery of similar interests (Kram & Isabella). Formal mentoring relationships usually involve a matching process that connects mentors and protégés for the purpose of strengthening careers and are often sponsored by various organizations (Kram & Isabella).

Combs (2003) suggested that African American women in leadership positions are forced into out-group status in terms of formal and informal networks because of the availability of these networks. Informal and formal networks are less accessible to African American women and may operate under different terms than that of Caucasian females and males (Combs). Combs study was a critical examination on the effect of the interaction of race and gender on informal networks of managerial African American women in organizations. The current study

24

is a critical examination of the effect of the interaction of race and gender on formal socialization networks (like that of mentoring) of African American women in leadership positions within Human Services.

The duality of race and gender for African American women managers/leaders is perceived to influence interaction in informal workplace socialization (Combs, 2003). Informal socialization systems facilitate access to career and social support (Combs). Combs asserted that these relationships greatly affect career opportunities and career advancement. A study conducted by the John T. Heldrich Center for Workplace Development (2002) indicated that workplace environments operate differently for African American women. The study also indicated that African American women are most likely perceived as being unfairly treated in terms of promotions and opportunities for training. Additionally, these women are further perceived to be more of a target for discrimination in the workplace. These perceived reasons affect African American women's access to participate in informal socialization networks.

The results of the John T. Heldrich Center for Workplace Development (2002) study coincide with the findings from Combs (2003) study. Both studies indicated that African American women in managerial or leadership positions do experience covert discrimination and subtle prejudice. These events lead to a lack of psychosocial support, contribute to failure, and reduce opportunity for participation in formal and informal networks such as mentoring. Combs (2003) recommended the need for further research to understand the experiences and career advancement opportunities of African American managers/leaders within organizational social systems or formal networks.

Social Network Groups

Friedman, Kane, and Cornfield's (1998) work on social network groups and race examined the strength of ties among African Americans that extend outside of employment, yet impact their careers and work attitudes. Unfortunately, there have only been a limited number of empirical studies that explore not only the differences between developmental networks of different racial groups, but also study the unique features of social networks within gender groups (Friedman, Kane, and Cornfield, 1998). The current study was an opportunity to develop race-specific or race-inclusive research of mentoring and career outcomes, as it relates to gender and race.

Racial Identity Development

Sheared (1994) introduced the idea of womanism and black women's epistemology. It offered a way of understanding the realities of a black woman's lived experiences. Black women's epistemology suggests that oppression has forced African American women to foster their own knowledge on meaning making systems (Sheared). Sheared implied that the standards used to assess and validate claims of knowledge rest on three premises: knowledge is gained from lived experiences; dialogue is used to account for knowledge claims; and a personal accountability of ethics is practiced. African American women believe in communicating their knowledge and doing what is morally right (Collins, 2000).

Helms (1990) defined Racial Identity Development theory as a group or collective identity. The premises of Racial Identity Development theory suggest that racial identity encompasses personal identity, group orientation, and associated identity (Helms). Group orientation is defined as the perception a person uses that associates them with a particular racial group. This group orientation guide feelings, thoughts, and behaviors (Helms). Even though many recognize the consequences of assigning individuals to racial categories, it is the most widely used tool of classification (Hewstone, Hantzi, & Johnston, 1991).

Although race and ethnicity are often used in reference to one another in literature, they should be treated as separate constructs (Helms, 1994; 1997). Helms posited that the two terms (race and ethnicity) have different conceptual meanings implying that race is politically and socially defined by racial classifications that are already set forth (Helms, 1996). On the other hand, Helms (1997) asserted that ethnicity is the derivative of cultural socialization and expression. According to Helms, the greatest difference surrounding the two constructs is that ethnicity is voluntary and race is not. One can choose their ethnicity, but they cannot choose their race. Race is given at birth and preordained.

Cross (1971) pointed out that African Americans went through several psychological changes because of their struggle with being systematically oppressed and dehumanized. The resultant model of Cross serves as a discovery of the psychological changes most minority groups go through while developing a positive group concept. The resultant model makes ethnic identity an important psychological construct to consider.

Phinney (1992) identified three psychological aspects of ethnicity: (a) group culture label; (b) ethnic identity; and (c) minority status. Culture refers to following or believing values, beliefs, behaviors, and norms associated with one's cultural group (Phinney). Ethnic identity refers to the extreme to which one identifies with his/her ethnic group - the meaning and strength of one's ethnic identity (Phinney). Minority status is the extent to which one has opposed experiences and attitudes associated with their minority status (Phinney). Phinney indicated that these attitudes are based on being a part of a minority group that is often the target of racist behaviors and prejudicial attitudes. African American women may be more equipped to mentor

27

other African American women because of the shared values associated with racial identity development.

Racial Identity and Organizational Success

Several companies in the United States have embraced the concept of diversity and recognize its impact on organizational success (Chen, Hickman, & Garcia, 2000). According to Chen, Hickman, and Garcia evidence of this can be found in the onset of initiatives that were started to attract and retain minorities and improve professional opportunities for women and people of color. The growing number of African Americans in the Unites States population challenge many organizations to work effectively with the emerging dynamics of cultural diversity (Grieco & Cassidy, 2001). Mentoring relationships, formal or informal, create conditions for organizational and personal success (Davidson & Foster-Johnson, 2001). It is critical for mentoring opportunities to be readily available for individuals of all races. Mentoring leads to leadership opportunities which eventually lead to personal growth and career advancement.

Mentoring relationships assist with integrating departments, cultivating essential professional and social networks, and set the foundation for advancement in the workforce (Davidson & Foster-Johnson, 2001). Bruce (1995) affirmed a lack of mentoring and guidance in their workplace among people of color especially women. It has been reported that it is more difficult for people of color to find mentors of the same race (Hansman, 2002).

A mentoring relationship is focused on the achievement of knowledge between the mentor and protégé (Colvin, 2010). An important component of this dynamic is the support and assistance provided by the mentor to the protégé. Oftentimes, the mentor helps the protégé achieve short and long-term goals (Colvin). Mentoring relationships are reciprocal and should

28

offer tangible benefits for both parties involved (Colvin). This exchange involves sharing information beyond what is documented and involves formal and informal components.

Davidson and Foster-Johnson (2001) stated that formal mentoring usually involves a third-party and the mentoring relationship usually last from six months to one year without frequent contact. It is usually focused on new employee orientation or career goals. On the contrary, Kram (1985) stated that informal relationships are unstructured and can last anywhere from three to six years. Informal mentoring relationships are focused on long-term goals (Kram). An individual may sometimes receive organizational recognition for their formal mentoring relationship, but are less likely to receive the intrinsic reward involved with informal mentoring (Kram).

In formal mentoring, organizations typically use matching systems to properly match a mentor and protégé. Informal mentoring involves a more experienced individual simply identifying the need to assist a less experienced individual with everyday decisions or life choices. Informal mentoring tends to be more personable than that of formal mentoring (Kram, 1985). Formal mentoring involves a shared goal between the mentor, the protégé, and the organization (Kram). Informal mentoring is a shared goal between the mentor and the protégé and does not involve a third party.

According to Ragins, Cotton, and Miller (2000), if formal mentoring programs incorporate components of informal mentoring, positive career outlooks, and job attitudes would be realized. Mentoring is an important process which has been linked to organizational success. It has also been linked to increased earnings, job satisfaction, access to more resources, and more successful careers (Dreher & Ash, 1990). There is increased evidence that mentoring programs produce positive results for people of color in the corporate world. For example, Cox and

29

Nkomo (1986) discovered that African American managers who had been mentored have experienced upward mobility faster than those who have not.

In the corporate world, most mentoring relationships described by persons are cross-gender and cross-race due to the large number of Caucasian men and women in organizational leadership positions (Dreher & Cox, 1996). There are studies that address the degree to which same-race partners affect the mentoring relationships, but the evidence obtained from these studies has been inconclusive and examined solely from the viewpoint of the protégé whose views of the relationship would be perceived differently than the mentor. The current study examined the attitudes and preference of same-race partners views from the mentor's perspective. The exchange that takes place between same-race partners in a mentoring relationship can be identified as a social exchange. Social Exchange Theory posits that individuals participate in a relationship because of a shared goal and chance for reciprocal benefit (Grossman & Rhodes, 2002).

Social Exchange Theory

Social Exchange theory has been defined as an ambitious socio-psychological theory (Zafirovski, 2005; Emerson, 1976). The evolution of Social Exchange theory stems back to Thorndike's (1932; 1935) work on the development of reinforcement theory and Mill's (1923) work on utility theory. Today's influences on Social Exchange theory are derived from sociologist's such as Homan (1950; 1961), Blau (1964), and Emerson (1972).

The model that has emerged to explain Social Exchange theory is composed of five key elements. These elements are,

- Behavior is associated with rationality. This means that the more rewards that are available for the behavior, the more often the behavior will be displayed.

- The relationship and reciprocation go hand in hand. This means that each individual involved in the relationship will provide benefits to the other as long as it is equitable for both.

- Justice principle directly affects the Social Exchange. In each exchange, there must be a component that ensures fairness during interaction between individuals.

- In the exchange relationship individuals want to maximize their gains and minimize their costs. Meaning individuals will seek to get the most out of the exchange. Cost does not necessarily represent a monetary component during the exchange. Cost is also in reference to time and effort invested.

- Mutual benefit is the key not coercion in the exchange relationship. Coercion during the exchange process should be minimal.

Zafirovski (2005) suggested that the sole premise of Social Exchange theory is that human behavior is an exchange of rewards between individuals. Emerson (1976) indicated that the exchange approach is the economic analysis of social situations that are non-economic. According to Stolte, Fine, and Cook (2001), Social Exchange theory allows an examination of large-scale social issues using the investigation of small-scale social situations.

An important component of Social Exchange theory is that it serves as a theoretical paradigm for social science. It is derived from the claim of the Rational Choice Model and Behaviorism (Stolte, Fine, & Cook, 2001). It is also an interdisciplinary approach that expounds boundaries of the social science disciplines between sociology, economics, psychology, and political science (Zafirovski, 2005). Homans (1961) posited that Social Exchange theory is based on the premise that human behavior or social interactions is an exchange of activity that can be either beneficial or non-beneficial. Zafirovski added that social exchange is done intentionally with certain predetermined targeted outcomes.

The interdependent processes within Social Exchange theory are the infrastructure or functioning mechanism within a definite social and institutional structure. These processes are governed by reciprocal relations (Emerson, 1969). The concept of ration exchange is lead by tools of power, dependence, and cohesion, and is reinforced in the attribute of reciprocal reinforcements (Emerson). Social Exchange theory examines the processes of establishing and maintaining reciprocity in social relations. It is also concerned with the mutual gratification between individuals (Zafirovski, 2005; Emerson). Mentors and protégés participate in a mentoring relationship for specific reasons such as reciprocal gains. This reasoning complies with the premises of Leader Member Exchange (LMX) theory which is an extension of Social Exchange Theory. Leader-Member Exchange Theory (LMX) is the exchange theory that supports the research design for this proposal.

Leader Member Exchange (LMX) Theory

Grossman and Rhodes (2002) stated that a relationship will only be successful if benefits of reciprocity exist within the relationship. Mentoring relationships are transformational and involve the mutual commitment of the mentor and protégé (Yukl, 1989). Leader-Member Exchange (LMX) theory is applicable to mentoring. LMX is a developmental relationship that consists of work related exchanges and interactions. Blau (1964) defined LMX as the focus on different interactional patterns between leaders and members of a group.

Dansereau, Graen, and Haga's (1975) approach to leadership was termed the Vertical

Dyad Linkage (VDL). The VDL model of leadership evolved to be most commonly called the Leader-Member Exchange model (LMX) (Schriesheim, Castro, & Cogliser, 1999). Graen and Uhl-Bien (1995) proved LMX has four (4) stages of development.

Stage one research found that leaders developed differential relationships with their subordinates (Schriesheim, Castro, & Cogliser, 1999). This was the opposite of previous leadership approaches that assumed leaders displayed consistent behavior toward all subordinates (Horner, 1997). The second stage focused on the differential relationships the leader had with subordinates (Schriesheim, Castro, & Cogliser). This began the examination of components surrounding the LMX construct. Graen and Uhl-Bien (1991) posited that the majority of LMX research has been conducted with a stage two focus. Graen and Uhl-Bien's Leadership Making model shifted LMX research into stage three and the emphasis shifted from examining the differential relationship between leader and subordinates to how leaders may work with each subordinate on a one-on-one basis in order to develop a unique partnership with each of them. The fourth stage widens the scope from the dyad to a larger perspective by exploring how dyadic relationships are organized within and beyond the organizational system (Schriesheim, Castro, & Cogliser, 1999).

LMX theory represents a transactional approach of how supervisors use their power and organizational resources for the development of exchange relationships with different subordinates (Scandura & Schriesheim, 1994). The cost benefit exchange between supervisors and subordinates suggests that supervisors are only committed to short-term development of their subordinates. An incorporation of the LMX concept with mentoring could substantially expand the boundaries of leader-member relationships. This expanse could potentially encourage subordinates to be more committed to the organization and the leaders once they understand how

33

satisfied their supervisors are because of their commitment (Scandura & Schriesheim). As a result, supervisors and managers could be more inclined to promote subordinates who demonstrate competencies in the area of leadership to leadership positions and encourage mentoring in the workplace.

Mentoring and Leadership Skills Competencies

The leader skills approach is more commonly used in Human Service leadership by managers because of its focus on identifying specific competencies (Scandura & Schriesheim, 1994). The leader skills approach implies that many people have leadership potential, and if they can learn from their experiences, they can become more effective leaders (Conway, 2002). This suggests that involvement with more experienced individuals will lead to an increase in skills, knowledge, and abilities. Mentoring relationships involve more experienced individuals passing knowledge to less experienced individuals thus, equipping the protégés with leadership skills competencies.

There has been past controversies associated with competencies in leadership development. Zenger and Folkman (2002) concluded that there are 16 competencies needed for organizational effectiveness. These characteristics include: display of honesty and integrity, technical and professional expertise, analytic ability to solve problems, innovation, self-development, results driven, setting goals, taking responsibility for outcomes, good communication, inspiring and motivating others, effectiveness of trust and interpersonal skills, concern for development of others, organizational change skills, and ability to relate well with superiors (Zenger & Folkman). From the competencies discussed here, it seems appropriate to infer that leaders make ideal mentors.

A mentor is defined as a more experienced individual who offers training to a less experienced individual (Hansman, 2002). Zenger and Folkman (2002) defined leadership as skills, traits, attributes, and knowledge that collectively assist an individual at performing their job. A leader, in turn, will have the opportunity to train a less experienced employee on how to effectively move into a future leadership position. This is an indication that mentoring could assist organizations in producing future leaders.

Leadership Development

Leadership has been described as one of the most researched phenomenon (Burns, 1978). According to Northouse (2004), leadership is a process by which an individual influences a group of individuals in an effort to achieve common goals. In Human Services, leaders come in the form of managers, directors, and supervisors. Their followers are those individuals leaders are attempting to influence. Oftentimes, the term follower is substituted or interchanged by the word subordinate (Bass, 1995). For the purpose of this study, therefore, subordinates will be described or represented as followers. The term follower gives the inference that leaders can be in any role or position and not subjected to the usual terms of hierarchy and/or bureaucracy (Packard, 2004). Gill (2006) characterized leadership as a quality of interactions, rather than an association of hierarchy levels.

Leadership is a key factor in coordinating and aligning organizational processes (Lewis, Packard, & Lewis, 2007). An organization must focus on organizational performance and desired outcomes in order to operate effectively and efficiently (Pulakos, 2012). A leader must possess certain qualities imperative to shape an organization's climate and culture (Packard, 2004). In order for a leader to lead appropriately, he/she must also be able to utilize leader-member processes and relevant follower characteristics with implementing best practices.

McNeece and Thyer (2004) suggested that evidence-based practice (EBP) methods should be used in the design and implementation of mentoring programs in Human Service agencies. They also suggested that using (EBP) to assess theories, models, and leadership guidelines for such agencies would make for best practices. Although leadership is sometimes viewed as a rational activity, it also has contextual implications. These implications include agency policy, political arena, and economic and social components (Lewis, Packard, & Lewis, 2007). Other contextual components are internal components such as, organizational power and politics (Lewis et al.).

In earlier examinations of leadership, it was affirmed that leaders possess specific traits that gave them the ability to lead (Packard, 2004). The trait approach suggests that leaders are born, not made. The leadership skills approach suggests that individuals can be taught to lead by other more experienced individuals or leaders. Fostering leadership skills approaches within Human Services organizations will require a strong infrastructure that includes leadership, material products, and human resources (Newhouse et al., 2002). It has been reported that best practices change models are used to assist and mentor project teams (Thurston & King, 2004). Research has shown that implementing leadership change models in organizations has been successful in transforming organizations strategically.

Mentoring is a leadership skills approach that has the ability to assist Human Service organizations in cultivating future leaders. One of the first steps in implementing mentoring is to establish a framework for building and maintaining the mentoring program (Thurston & King, 2004). There ought to be committees in place to address how the program will be fostered. The committee must include committee chairs, standards of practice, quality assurance, staff

36

education, and research (Thurston & King). The committee goals should align with the goals of implementing the mentoring program (Thurston & King, 2004). During the implementation process, the committee chairs have direct responsibility in assuring their committee is aligned with completion of the set forth agency goals.

One of the most important steps of the program is the development of experts that can serve as mentors. These mentors are the primary champions and facilitators of the program (Thurston & King, 2004). These are the members of the governance committees that are responsible for incorporating leadership best practices goals and moving the organization strategically forward. There are a number of material resources necessary for implementing a mentoring program. These resources include: a leader-member exchange model to follow, a process, guidelines, and experienced individuals (Thurston & King). Training and mentoring should be offered through experienced committee members who have expressed interest in mentoring. In contrast, although having previous experience in mentoring would be a plus, for some individuals, it may be their first opportunity to mentor or participate in a mentoring relationship, and prove to be just as beneficial.

There are also three (3) limitations to consider when dealing with workplace mentoring in relation to mentoring best practices. The first limitation is that workplace mentoring is often viewed as a one-sided relationship leading to instrumental outcomes (Ragins & Verbos, 2007). This means that the mentor serves as a protector of his/her protégé. The mentor can be prone to offer favors and in return, expect allegiance from the protégé. The second limitation indicates that narrow lenses have been used to assess mentoring outcomes (Ragins & Verbos). For example, most available literature on mentoring outcomes has been measured or based on work and career compensation and work attributes as received by the protégé. The third limitation is that current mentoring literature does not include cognitive and effective processes that underlie effective mentoring relationships (Ragins & Verbos). Current literature has not addressed mutual relational behavior and relational outcomes. The current study examined this reciprocal exchange from the view of the mentor. The current study can be compared to previous studies done from the view of the protégé to allow for a comparison analysis.

Conclusion

In examining the theory associated with this proposal, it was necessary to trace the history of the LMX concept. It is apparent that the theoretical content of LMX has varied during the evolution of leadership theories and is a direct extension of Social Exchange Theory. Leadership theories were dormant until 1975 when Haga, Graen, and Dansereau began the movement towards paradigms that employed constructs of Social Exchange Theory. The research by Dansereau et al. (1975) and Graen and Cashman (1975) furthered developed the definition of Social Exchange Theory and began the evolution toward Leader Member Exchange Theory (LMX). The current proposal furthered research on LMX by examining the social exchange between the leader (mentor) and the subordinate (protégé) by the view of the mentor (the leader).

Leader Member Exchange Theory (LMX) and Racial Identity Development are necessary components that needed to be examined when taking into consideration the attitudes and preferences in mentoring of African American women in Human Service leadership to adequately understand their perceptions. The literature review for this study focused on race and gender as they relate to the mentoring relationship. The components examined in this literature review will offer insight and understanding on the results gathered from this study.

CHAPTER 3. METHODOLOGY

The previous literature review assisted in establishing the theoretical context for the study. The purpose of this chapter is to present the qualitative research methodology that was employed to approach the research questions. The purpose of this current study, as aforementioned, is to address a gap in the mentoring literature by examining mentoring relationships among African American women in Human Service leadership. The next section focuses on the different aspects of the research design: sample, instrumentation, measures, data collection, data analysis, validity and reliability, and ethical considerations. To examine the attitudes and preferences of African American women in Human Service leadership, the following research questions guided this investigation:

RQ1: How do African American women mentors in Human Service leadership select their protégés?

RQ2: What are the attitudes of African American women in Human Service leadership, regarding the effect of mentoring on their career advancement?

Research Design

Research is philosophical and used by scholar-practitioners to expand their knowledge in specific paradigms of their choosing. This study used a generic qualitative methodology. According to Swanson and Holton (2005), research studies are the most prevalent aspects of phenomena that choreograph specific events or points in time. It is through previous research that philosophical assumptions of scholar-practitioners are applied. In turn, these assumptions guide future studies. When considering methodology for research design, there are three (3) key methodological assumptions: ontological, axiological, and epistemological.

.

Ontological

Ontological assumptions are the researcher's perceptions of reality. It must be objective. Assumptions for this study were objective and post-positivist. Post-positivism is based on determination, reductionism, and empirical observation (Creswell, 2009). Creswell further added that post-positivism focuses on collecting data to support or refute a theory.

Axiological

Creswell (2009) pointed out that axiological foundations are based on the values of the researcher. Creswell also suggested that a researcher acts in a value free and unbiased manner when conducting a study. Research was conducted in an unbiased manner throughout the entire study including the data collection process. An axiological assumption made at the beginning of this study was that there would be a number of reasons why mentors select their protégés the way they do. Another assumption was that there would be diverse views concerning whether mentors believe mentoring will affect their own career advancement.

Epistemological

Researchers are independent from the concepts or variables under the study (Creswell, 2009). The epistemological assumption for this study was that there would be a number of diverse reasons for mentor protégé selection and for their perceptions of mentoring on career advancement. Each mentor's lived experiences as a mentor contributed to the epistemological findings in this study.

Qualitative Research Methodology

Qualitative research approach is subjective and derives from exploring the manner in which people construe their experiences (Denzin & Lincoln, 2005; Creswell, 2003). The methodology utilizes a pragmatic and rational viewpoint to explore human experiences (Vishnevsky & Beanlands, 2004). Qualitative research is essential in comprehending the ontological perceptions of individuals' natural environments (Creswell; Barbuto, 2005). In essence, qualitative research is relevant to understand the beliefs of differing actualities concerning the opinions of each individual (Wilding &Whiteford, 2005; Hesse-Biber & Leavy, 2005).

According to Donalek (2004), the results obtained through qualitative research produce understanding and awareness. The truths which emerge from utilizing a qualitative research methodology are explicit to context or situation since the results may not extend further than the group that is being studied. Qualitative research, therefore, generates information about individuals who may not be naturally heard and permits realities to emerge from the entire group (Donalek; Ruane, 2005).

In preparation for this study, a review of the mentoring literature found that mentoring scholars chose quantitative methods of research to assess relationships between mentoring variables. Studies which have used a quantitative research method to assess relationships among mentor variables include: Ragins and Cotton (1993) - a regression analysis was used to determine chance effects variables had upon each other; Niehoff (2006) – a study on the personality characteristics of mentors which examined the relationship between personality and participation as a mentor; and Tonidaniel, Avery, and Phillips (2007) - an investigation of the

41

impact of protégé performance after the mentor relationship was done by examining the relationship between mentor success and protégé performance. Few studies involving African American female mentors exist. Thus, the understanding of the experiential aspects of female African American mentors in leadership positions is missing.

Generic Qualitative Approach

The philosophic assumption for this study was objective and post-positivist. For this study, a generic qualitative research methodology was used because of missing experiential literature on female African American mentors in leadership positions. Baxter and Jack (2008) implied that the generic qualitative design is a research approach that explores a phenomenon within its context. This approach allows the issue to be explored through the lenses of the research participants.

Caelli and Miller (2003) posit that generic qualitative approaches seek to discover and understand a phenomenon, a process, or the perspectives and worldviews of the people involved. Caelli and Miller suggest that researchers using a generic approach should make their theoretical position clear, and the analytical lens through which their data was examined should be identified. Generic qualitative studies tend not to use a traditional qualitative approach (ethnography, phenomenology, etc.) and take a general approach toward clinical issues.

Key considerations in using a generic approach are concerns with the creation of a convincing account or study (Cooper & Endacott, 2007). The need for clarity in relation to validity and reliability are very important. Instead of credibility and dependability, respondent validation and reflexivity are important when using generic approaches (Cooper & Endacott). Three key areas of importance when considering generic approaches are: reflexivity, establishing rigour, and methods (Cooper & Endacott).

Reflexivity

Cooper and Endacott (2007) define reflexivity as sensitivity to the ways the researcher and the research process have shaped the collection of data. This research process includes the researcher's assumptions and prior experiences. Caelli and Miller (2003) argued that it is important for a qualitative researcher to make clear and define their theoretical position with specific regards to their disciplinary affiliation.

The theoretical framework for this study is Leader-Member Exchange theory (LMX) and Racial Identity Development theory. LMX focuses on the relationship between the superior and the group or subordinate. Each linkage is suggested to differ in quality. The leader may have poor inter-personal relations with some subordinates, but will be open and trusting with others. In essence, the leader provides support, consideration, and assistance mandated by duty, but will not go beyond these limits (Lunerburg, 2010). By aligning LMX theory with mentoring, this study contributed to concepts of LMX theory. There was a gap in the literature on LMX Theory as it relates to mentoring and African American females. The results of this study aligned with concepts of LMX theory and examined LMX's influence on mentoring relationships among African American women in Human Service leadership.

Racial Identity Development theory focuses on the collective attributes of a group that exists and identity of the group. These attributes include: beliefs, values, habits, lived experiences, and attitudes. Collaboratively, Racial Identity Development theory can explain the attitudes and preferences of a particular group (Cross, 1991). This study contributed to concepts of Racial Identity Development Theory by offering insight on the attitudes and preferences in mentoring among African American females.

Establishing Rigour

Cooper and Endacott (2007) suggest that when considering a generic qualitative study and in order to produce a convincing account, researchers need to keep clear and accurate records and describe the research process in detail. They described this in-depth research process as "the audit trail." Cooper and Endacott suggest that this audit trail will allow the reader to consider the relevance of the findings to other settings, and will also enhance validity and reliability.

Methods

Cooper and Endacott (2007) suggest methods be described in full with consideration to sampling, interviews, observation, and analysis. Cooper and Endacott described random sampling as unusual in qualitative research. Random sampling was not used for this study. For this study, there was a targeted population, African American women in Human Service leadership positions.

Sample

Qualitative study sample size is generally smaller than those used in quantitative studies (Ritchie, Lewis, & Elam, 2003). The sample size must be large enough to assure that most or all of the perceptions covered are relevant and important. However, the sample must not be so large that data becomes repetitive and irrelevant (Mason, 2010). Creswell (1998) suggested that sample size for qualitative research range from 5 to 25 participants and at least 6 to conduct an efficient study. For this study, the targeted and achieved sample size was 10. Saturation was achieved with this sample size.

Instrumentation/Measures

This study is a Generic Qualitative Study. Six (6) demographic questions were asked on the first page of the open-ended interview questions to provide information regarding the sample (See Appendix A). The open-ended questionnaire was answered in a face-to-face semi-structured interview that was tape recorded for accuracy and coding purposes. The recordings were transcribed by the researcher and immediately destroyed after transcription. Questions 1-3 on the open-ended questionnaire offered information on how African American women select their protégés (See Appendix B). Questions 4-6 offered information on how mentors see protégé selection will affect their career advancement (See Appendix B). The information gathered was descriptive and came from the mentors lived experiences (See Table 1 below).

Table 1. Layout of Research Questions

Research Questions	Questions Number
ResQ1 – Preferences for African American women mentors regarding protégé selection	1, 2, 3
ResQ2 - The attitudes of African American women in Human Service leadership, regarding the effect of mentoring on their career advancement	4, 5, 6

Field Test

Cooper and Schindler (2008) stated that validity represents the degree to which an

45

instrument measures the intended measures. Lincoln and Guba (1985) affirmed that validity represents the degree to which the research findings accurately describe reality. The validity and reliability of the instrument used for this study were confirmed by a field test. The interview questions for this study were examined by three (3) supervisors who are knowledgeable in the field of mentoring. The three (3) supervisors who participated in this field test had over 30 years of combined experience in mentoring. The interview questions designed for this study were affirmed to have the ability to elicit the desired information needed for the study; no changes were recommended to the questions by any of the reviewers.

Data Collection

As previously mentioned, the sample for this study was drawn from a non-profit organization in Midwest United States. This organization employs several African American women who are or have been mentors. It creates opportunities for non-able and able individuals to gather education and training for inclusion into the workforce. The members of this organization, including African American women, participate in mentoring on a formal and informal level daily.

The most common source of data collection in qualitative research is interviews, observations, and review of documents (Creswell, 2009). Of these sources, interviews are the most common form practiced. For this study, interviews were conducted and tape recorded. The use of a digital recording is a qualitative methodology good practices component because it preserves the entire verbal part of the interview for later analysis. The downside to using a tape recorder revolves around malfunctioning equipment. To ensure that the tape recorder operated properly, the researcher made sure that the recorder had new batteries at all times. Extra packs of batteries were on hand at all times. The tape recorder was also stopped and played back to ensure the recorder was working properly early in the interview. The tape recorder was also played back at the beginning of the interview to make sure the interviewee was speaking loudly into the microphone and could be clearly heard. At the end of the interview, the interviewee was thanked and no future contact was necessary after the study was completed.

For this study, interviews with open-ended questions were used and tape recorded. Since site approval had been granted by the Program Coordinator, once IRB approval was received, the recruitment and data collection process began. The Coordinator provided a recruitment flyer via email to the organization's entire staff. The researcher's contact information was available on the flyer and potential participants contacted the researcher to set up dates and times for one-on-one interview sessions. Once the researcher was contacted, the potential participants were screened to ensure they met the eligibility requirements, e.g., African American females who have mentored or were currently mentoring. After eligibility had been determined, a date and time was set up for the interview to be conducted at the organization.

At the beginning of the interview, the informed consent process was reviewed step by step. Once the informed consent document was discussed in depth and the participant acknowledged that they understood, agreed, and were willing to participate in the study, the document was signed by the participant and the researcher. A copy of the signed informed consent form was given to the participant. The tape recorder was started and the interview began. Interviews lasted from 45 minutes to an hour. Participants were then thanked for their time and presented with a $25 Red Lobster gift card as a token of appreciation for their participation. There was no further contact with the participant, but they were informed that a copy of the completed study will be provided to the organization upon receipt of Capella University approval which they could obtain if they were interested in reviewing the study results.

Data Analysis

Coding, categorizing, data reduction and emergent themes were the methods used for data analysis (See Table 2 and Table 3). The information gathered from the interviews was first transcribed and the tape recordings were immediately destroyed. For this study, a military pseudonym was utilized to identify participants. The interviewees were labeled as Alpha, Bravo, Charlie, Echo, etc. The transcribed information for each newly renamed participant was put into distinct categories by dissecting each interview and identifying similarities through the process of data reduction and coding. Coding is the process of organizing and sorting data. Codes served as a way to label, condense and organize the data collected. After data collection was complete, each individual interview questions data was pooled to find themes to answer the research questions. RQ1 was answered from interview questions 1-3, and RQ2 was answered from interview questions 4-6 (See Table 1).

Miles and Huberman (1994) indicated that the process of creating codes is a good practice when analyzing data. Emergent codes are those ideas, concepts, actions, relationships, and meanings that come up in the data and are different than the pre-set codes. Emergent codes appeared as the researcher analyzed the data. Emergent codes (or themes) were used for the data analysis of this study (See Table 4).

As data was being coded, the coding scheme was refined by creating specific categories for those schemes that were similar (See Table 4). The information was added, collapsed, expanded, and revised using a thematic coding and categorizing method (Gibbs, 2007). The main thing the researcher did when coding the data was to ensure that the codes were made to fit the data, rather than trying to make the data fit the codes. While conducting the data analysis for this study, codes began to repeat themselves frequently for some of the research questions. These codes were identified by focusing on key words and phrases. It was at this point that the researcher realized saturation had been achieved.

Coding was employed to translate the information from interviews and tape recordings. Coding is the process of examining the qualitative data which will be in the form of words, phrases, sentences or paragraphs, and assigning codes or labels (Corbin & Strauss, 1990). Corbin and Strauss identified two types of coding: axial coding and open coding; both types were used in the analysis of this study's data. Open coding involves words and phrases found in the transcript or text. Some of the words and phrases that were found in the transcripts of interviews that seemed to repeat were 'organizational requirements', 'willingness to learn', 'personal growth', and 'identifiable experience' (See Table 2). Axial coding then involves the creation of themes or categories by grouping codes or labels given to words and phrases. There were four (4) themes identified as a result of this coding process. These themes will be discussed fully in Chapter 4.

Table 2. Quotes from Participants

Name	Question 1	Question 2	Question 3	Question 4	Question 5	Question 6
Alpha	"Past experiences, desired outcomes, organization (formal - involuntary)"	"Likes, dislikes, needs, goals, common experiences, organizational requirements (formal – involuntary)"	"If mentor can't commit More harm than good would result"	"Mentor need to go further and try to do better Mentor may not be suitable"	"It's beneficial, professional growth, personal growth"	"When you do good things good things happen, when you mentor it gives the protégé the desire to mentor someone else"
Bravo	"Organization (formal-involuntary)"	"Barriers that hinder their success; ex. Basic skills, demographics, incarcerated parents, etc."	"If mentors safety is a concern"	"Makes mentor want to try harder or think outside the box"	"Their self-esteem is built, given more tools, open up what they know about careers, makes mentor test professional limits"	"Personal fulfillment knowing your helping someone who may not have made it that far without you, faith based, thrilling"
Charlie	"When someone displays they are in need of guidance and hungry to learn"	"Want to learn, open to constructive criticism, willing to take things they are learning and infuse them in their own lives"	"Protégé is not open to suggestions, someone who wants to play the role of the victim, age or immaturity"	"Can only affect it negatively for the protégé, people at work already know you"	"It would affect career advancement by showing your leadership qualities"	"To see the protégé grow, mature, and further themselves, to see them achieve what they thought was not achievable gives a feeling of fulfillment"
Delta	"Organization (formal – involuntary) "	"Someone in need of guidance, someone who wants help but don't know what steps to take"	"There is no one I would consider not mentoring"	"Would give more attention, would make them see I practice what I preach, service is the key"	"Everyone needs someone to guide them, helps career advancement, mentoring helped me as a protégé"	"To help someone think twice is personal fulfillment, a positive outlook on life"

Table 2. Quotes from Participants *continued*

Name	Question 1	Question 2	Question 3	Question 4	Question 5	Question 6
Echo	*"Self motivated, eager to learn, sense of pride"*	"Certain amount of education or experience, someone who knows how to think outside the box"	"When the person feels they have all the knowledge they need or don't need a mentor"	"Does not affect professional reputation"	"Has a lot to do with career advancement, sometimes people are mentoring and don't know it"	"Expands you personally, self-fulfilling goal, and gives you a feeling of success"
Foxtrot	"Identifiable experiences, have experienced the same things"	"Barriers that hinder their success"	"Nothing would make me not mentor, try my best to help everyone"	*"Should help my professionalism"*	"Personally feel it should be incorporated in every position in Human Services"	"Should not be a physical reward, makes me feel good to hear them say I was part of their success, personal fulfillment"
Golf	"Organization (formal – involuntary) "	"Barriers that hinder their success"	"Would not consider not mentoring , if the protégé is not showing engagement or commitment I would offer other resources"	"It can be helpful, will try harder, will identify what I need to do to reach the protégé, would not give up, would try another way"	"Positive effect on career advancement because I want to do this, passion speaks for itself"	"Seeing someone progress and do a good job makes me feel good, it's a personal reward"
Hotel	"Someone who needs additional support, someone who clings to me that I build a connection with"	"Aspirations, want to go to college, someone who wants and needs guidance"	*"Clashing personalities, does not respect me or my beliefs"*	"Does not affect my professional reputation, prefer low performing because they have a greater need for support"	"Gives me real life experience to apply in the workplace, apply knowledge in career field"	"Personal gratification, I feel I'm changing the world one person at a time"
India	"Someone in need"	"Sincerity and committed, desire to receive help"	"When they don't want the help being offered"	"Does not affect my professional reputation, not concerned with reputation when mentoring"	"Big effect on career advancement, gives me a bigger stepping stone"	"Personal fulfillment, the reward is seeing them achieve"

Table 2. Quotes from Participants *continued*

Name	Question 1	Question 2	Question 3	Question 4	Question 5	Question 6
Juliet	"Someone in need of guidance and support, organization (formal – involuntary) "	"In need of help, willing to accept assistance"	"Would never consider not mentoring"	"Should not affect professional reputation if carrying regular work habits into mentoring relationship, your reputation would stay the same"	"Affects career advancement in a positive way because it shows your willing to support organizational growth"	"Gives a feeling of personal achievement, helping others is the right thing to do, knowledge is to be shared not hidden away"

Note: Findings in italic are those responses that did not follow the pattern of emerging codes.

Ethical Considerations

When conducting research involving human participants, there are three (3) core ethical principles that need to be followed at all times respect for persons, beneficence, and justice.

Respect for Persons

Respect for persons involves ensuring the autonomy of the research participants. This includes protecting people from exploitation where autonomy is diminished (Denzin & Lincoln, 2000). The dignity of the research participants was respected at all times while conducting this study. The principle 'Respect for Persons,' was applied at all times throughout the study. Interviews were first scheduled at a time that was convenient for the participants; the location (e.g., a conference room at the workplace) was also selected to provide optimal convenience for

52

the participant. Verbal communications were used to inform participants of their right to withdraw from the study at any time. Additionally, as mentioned earlier, tape recordings were destroyed immediately after transcribing the interviews. Data from the interviewed was transcribed and coded using a military pseudonym system and labeled such as Alpha, Bravo, Charlie, and so forth to protect participant confidentiality.

Beneficence

Beneficence ensures that the researcher minimizes any risk associated with conducting the study. This ethical consideration includes minimizing psychological and social risks. Beneficence also suggests that researchers maximize the benefits that accrue to the research participants. It is important for researchers to also articulate how this will be achieved to the participants. In this study, it was explained to the participants the relativity of the study. They were also informed of the importance of the study and how and why it would assist with furthering research on mentoring. Participants were again offered the option of declining to participate in the study without consequence during the informed consent process.

Justice

Justice requires a fair distribution of the risks and benefits resulting from the research. Denzin and Lincoln (2000) stated that those who take on the burdens of research participation should share in the benefits of the knowledge reproduced. During the interviews, participants were given a $25 gift card in consideration for their time for participating in the study. The publication will also be made available to the organization upon its completion and approval by Capella University.

Chapter Summary

For this chapter, the research method and design, data collection, data analysis, validity and reliability of the research instrument, and ethical considerations were discussed. This study used a generic qualitative research methodology. Data analysis was done through the process of data reduction, coding, and categorization of emergent themes. Chapters 4 will discuss the findings, including the emergent themes. Chapter 5 will discuss these findings as they relate to the literature, and implications for practice and theory. This chapter will also discuss the study limitations, suggestions for future studies, and conclusions.

CHAPTER 4. RESULTS

This qualitative study was designed to explore and examine the attitudes and preferences regarding protégé selection and the effect mentoring has on career advancement in African American women mentors. The qualitative methodology provided a developmental framework whereby studying mentoring attitudes and preferences of African American women could be done. The framework presented described the data collection, data analysis, and interview instrument used to collect data for this study.

Chapter 4 provides an analysis and interpretation of the data collected from one-on-one interview sessions. Demographics for this study are discussed, the research questions are reintroduced, and a thorough interpretation of the study's results are given. Further interpretation of the findings, results of the data, and recommendations for future research will be discussed in Chapter 5.

Research Questions

The following research questions were employed to guide the study concerning the attitudes and preferences of African American women mentors:

RQ1: How do African American women mentors in Human Service leadership select their protégés?

RQ2: What are the attitudes of African American women in Human Service leadership, regarding the effect of mentoring on their career advancement?

Site Description

The organization selected for this research study was a nonprofit organization headquartered in Midwest United States. The organization is a non-profit organization that provides job opportunities for able and disabled individuals. It offers many programs such as career counseling, skills training, mentoring, education and literacy programs, and employment services. The organization was incorporated in October 1940 as an Employment and Vocational Service to help those in greatest need by providing desired employment and community services. This organization was selected because it has over 100 African American women from various social sectors who are currently or who have participated in workplace mentoring.

Description of Sample

Creswell (1998) suggest that sample size for qualitative methodologies range from 5 to 25 participants and at least six (6) to conduct an efficient study. This study aimed for ten (10) participants to help ensure saturation and this sample size was achieved. It was at the point when results became saturated that the researcher concluded that an adequate sample size had been achieved.

As previously indicated, the research participants consisted of 10 African American women mentors who work in Human Service leadership positions. The participants contacted the researcher and self identified to participate in the study. The women who participated in this study provided demographics based on age, highest level of education completed, length of time at current organization, length of time in current position, and length of time as a mentor (See Table 3).

In an effort to recruit respondents, a recruitment flyer was emailed to the Coordinator of the organization. The recruitment flyer was emailed after site permission was granted and IRB approval was received. After receiving the recruitment flyer from the researcher, the Coordinator sent the email to the organization's entire staff. The African American women that fit the research criteria outlined on the recruitment flyer and were interested in participating in the study contacted the researcher by the contact information provided on the recruitment flyer.

Upon initial contact, the individuals were screened to ensure they met the inclusion criteria for this study (e.g., African American women in Human Service leadership positions who have been a mentor or whom are currently mentoring). After it was confirmed that the potential participants met the inclusion criteria, a date and time was set up for the interview session. The interviews were held at the organization's main headquarters in a private conference room on the agreed upon dates and times.

At the beginning of each interview, the Informed Consent form was presented and reviewed. The researcher reviewed the document with each participant to address any questions that the participant may have and to obtain her decision to participate in the study. After reviewing the Informed Consent form, the researcher asked the participant if they understood and agreed to the information presented on the form. Once the participant acknowledged that they agreed and understood the information set forth on the Informed Consent document and were interested in participating in the study, two copies of the form was signed by the participant and researcher; one signed copy was retained by the researcher, while the other was provided to the participant.

Results of the demographic information collected for this study indicated that the research participants' ages ranged from 27 to 62 years (See Table 3). The highest level of education completed among the participants was a Master's degree. The combined Human Service experience for the participants was 66 years (See Table 3). However, combined mentoring experience for the participants was 136 years (See Table 3). Each participant had also been employed at the current organization for over two (2) years.

Table 3. Demographics

Demographics	Participant Information
Age in years	20-29 = 2 30-39 = 3 40-49 = 2 50-59 = 2 60-69 = 1
Highest level of education	High School Diploma = 2 Associate's degree = 1 Bachelor's degree = 5 Master's degree = 2 PhD = 0
Length of time in current position in years	0-10 = 8 11-20 = 0 21-30 = 1 31-40 = 1
Length of time in current organization in years	0-10 = 7 11-20 = 3 21-30 = 0
Type of Industry	Human Services = 10
Length of time mentoring in years	0-10 = 5 11-20 = 3 21-30 = 1 31-40 = 0 41-50 = 1

Research Methodology Applied to Data Collection and Analysis

The information collected was coded and each interviewee was assigned a military pseudonym to protect confidentiality. The military pseudonym used to describe the 10 participants was assigned alphabetically, e. g., Alpha, Bravo, Charlie, Delta, etc. The research questions for this study were answered using a generic qualitative research methodology. Data reduction, coding, categorization, and emergent themes allowed the researcher to concluded findings substantial for the research questions set forth. In relation to their respective questions on the interview instrument, interview questions 1-3 provided data for research question 1, and interview questions 4-6 provided the necessary data for research question 2.

Analysis, Synthesis, and Findings

Interview Question #1

Explain your process for selecting a protégé?

Responses to the first question reflected a need for help as the main reason a mentor would choose to help a protégé as stated by Charlie, Hotel, India, and Juliet. Charlie stated, "When someone displays they are in need of guidance and hungry to learn it makes me want to assist them." Hotel's comments were similar to Charlie's. Hotel commented, "Someone who needs additional support and someone who clings to me that I build a connection with." India stated in three (3) simple words, "Someone in need." And, Juliet explained, "Someone in need of guidance and support or someone my organization appoints me to mentor." Need for help can either be self-identified by the possible protégé or if the mentor could tell, by observation, that the possible protégé needed help. Organizational (formal) responsibility was also identified as a reason for selecting a protégé as stated by Alpha, Bravo, Delta, and Juliet. Alpha stated, "Past experiences, desired outcomes, and organizational appointment would prompt me to mentor someone. Organizational appointment may be the one that is the hardest to deal with because it is involuntary. Your company just pairs you with a protégé they think may be ideal for you to mentor." Bravo commented, "My organization picks who they want us to mentor in most circumstances. I still mentor individuals who need mentoring on a daily basis that have not been assigned to me though. I love mentoring and it is very personal for me." Delta explained,

"When protégés are assigned by my organization I mentor them." If their mentoring responsibility was associated with their job, the selection of their protégé was done for them. Formal mentoring programs, like the ones offered in organizations, use a matching system to connect mentors and protégés. This process is done with the belief that the matching system will ensure success.

Although eight out of 10 participants suggested need for help and organizational responsibility as the main reasons for selecting a protégé among African American women in Human Service leadership, identifiable experiences was also given as a plausible reason for protégé selection as stated by Alpha and Foxtrot. Foxtrot commented, "Someone I can identify with and have experienced the same things will make a better fit than mentoring someone I cannot identify with." Identifiable experience was defined as those elements that were present in a possible protégé's life that the mentor could identify with because of personal experience. Although identifiable experiences were mentioned, the response was not given enough to suggest it played a significant part in the protégé selection process. However, Alpha shared, "When you identify with someone you tend to mentor them whether it's required or not. Many of us mentor everyday and on a regular basis because it's in our nature." Alpha went on to state, "If it had not been for the mentors in my life I may not be where I am today."

Interview Question #2

What components or qualities does a protégé need to possess to be selected?

For this interview question Alpha, Bravo, Foxtrot and Golf stated that barriers that hinder success would be a component a possible protégé would need to possess. When the respondents were asked what would be considered barriers to success, several answers were provided. Foxtrot shared, "Barriers could be programmatic requirements that the organization sets forth for its mentoring program or personal barriers that are just present in a possible protégé's life. Programmatic and personal barriers are single-parenting, school drop-out, incarcerated parent, and/or low-income household." Alpha stated, "Generally likes, dislikes, needs, goals, common experiences. Official barriers would be programmatic or organizational requirements. Unofficial requirements would be the needs, desires, and common experiences." Bravo shared, "Programmatic barriers like basic skills deficiency, zip code, or incarcerated parents."

Charlie and Delta commented that someone who wants help or displays they need help, as a quality protégé's need to possess to be selected. When Charlie and Delta were asked to explain how they identify someone who needs help, Delta shared, "That someone who needs help will be open to constructive criticism and they will also be eager to learn about the mentoring process and will want to know exactly what is expected of them. They will be on-time and attentive during the entire mentoring program or process. Additionally, they will verbally tell me in advance, "I Need Help" or "Will You Help Me."

Interview Question #3

What are some things that would make you consider not mentoring a possible protégé?

Responses to this research question revealed that there are not a lot of things that could influence an African American woman not to mentor. The two reasons given by all respondents except Bravo were (a) the protégé did not want to be mentored and (b) they would never consider not being a mentor. When the researcher asked respondents to elaborate on how they would determine the protégé doesn't want to be mentored, Echo shared, "If the protégé does not want to listen to advice from the beginning and felt they knew everything. You have a lot of protégés who don't see the potential you see in them. In cases like this the mentoring experience would be ineffective because the protégé is closed off from the start. You can only mentor individuals that want to be mentored." Bravo is the only respondent who answered this question differently than the other respondents. Bravo shared, "If my safety is a concern I would definitely consider not mentoring." When the researcher asked Bravo to explain further, she stated, "Some of the protégés we are given to mentor require visits to their homes and they often times live in dangerous areas. It is during these times when I have to consider my safety and I may ask them to meet me in a public place rather than their homes and if they choose not to, I would have to consider not mentoring them."

When the respondents were asked to elaborate on their answer, (2) they would never consider not mentoring, the responses given were enlightening. Alpha shared, "If I can't fully commit to the mentoring relationship and it will do more harm than good I would consider not mentoring." Foxtrot stated firmly, "There is nothing that would make me consider not mentoring because if it had not been for the mentors in my life, I would not be where I am today." Foxtrot contributed much, if not all, of her success to the mentoring bestowed on her in the past.

Interview Question #4

How does being a mentor to a low performing protégé affect your professional reputation?

The responses for this question definitely shed light on the preferences of African American women mentors. There were two main conclusions drawn from this question: (1) African American women do not feel low performing protégés will have any effect on their career advancement and (2) they prefer low performing protégés. When the respondents were asked to elaborate on why they prefer low performing protégés, Alpha, Bravo, Delta, and Golf responded that low performing protégés make them want to try harder to reach the participant. Delta shared, "I prefer the protégés that are hard to reach or inner-city protégés because I was an inner-city protégé. You have to practice what you preach with low performing protégés. Service is the key." Bravo stated, "It allows me to step outside the box or outside my comfort zone and try other ways to reach the protégé. If a protégé is low performing, maybe the techniques being used by me are not effective for that particular protégé. Each mentoring experience is different. Techniques used with one protégé, may not prove to be effective with another. Working with low performing protégés makes me step my game up, because failure is not an option." Alpha stated, "If they are low performing does it mean they are not receiving it, or does it mean I need to go further or does it mean they may need a more suitable mentor? It would push me to do better and find out what the protégé really needs." Golf shared, "I don't think it affect it negatively. I believe it can be helpful. Sometimes you have to possess certain qualities to reach a protégé. You may need to identify what things may be going on that may be hindering you. It would enhance my reputation because I don't give up and I would keep going until I reach them. It's important for the protégé to see you don't give up. If they constantly see people giving up, it may contribute to their lack of motivation."

Interview Question #5

Explain the affect mentoring, if any, has on career advancement?

When respondents were asked this mentoring question, saturation was reached a little quicker than with the other questions. All respondents believed that participating in mentoring relationships offered them professional growth and enhanced their leadership qualities. When asked to elaborate on these responses, Charlie shared, "Participating in formal mentoring

63

programs with my organization allows my leadership abilities to be displayed. This, in turn, will hopefully create opportunities for promotions and future mentoring engagements. Since my organization knows they can depend on me, they have given me more responsibilities." Alpha stated, "It's beneficial for me in a professional and a personal way. It extends pass the organization into my personal life and I am able to use the same soft skills that are applied in mentoring to my personal life." Bravo answered this question in reference to protégés career advancement and mentors, "Their self-esteem is built and their given more tools. It opens up what they know about careers. It makes mentors test their professional limits." Delta stated, "Everyone needs someone to guide them and it helps my career advancement. A mentoring program helped me when I was in need of guidance, a protégé." Foxtrot exclaimed, "I personally feel it should be incorporated in every position in Human Services." Hotel commented, "It gives me real life experiences to apply in the workplace and I like apply life experiences in my career field." India commented, "Mentoring has a big effect on career advancement because it shows I can care for others. It also gives me a bigger stepping stone."

Interview Question #6

What type of fulfillment is achieved from being a mentor?

Responses to this question reached saturation quicker than with any other question in this study. In one way are the other, the responses to this question all ended up in the same ball park. Personal fulfillment was the main reason given for reward achieved from mentoring. When respondents were asked to elaborate on what type of personal fulfillment was achieved, Alpha, Bravo, Charlie, Echo, Foxtrot, and Golf reflected on when they were mentors. Alpha stated, "It's a reasonable service because no knowledge or experience is for personal benefit.

Sometimes the best learning is through bi-curious learning. When you do good then good comes in return. When you mentor someone they have the want or instinct to mentor in the future." Bravo stated, "I get a thrill from it. To understand you're helping someone who may not have made it that far without you. I feel blessed to be able to help someone. It is faith based for me." Charlie exclaimed, "The best reward is to see that person grow, mature, and further themselves. To see them achieve something that they thought was unachievable. Even if its baby steps, it's achievement toward a bigger picture." Delta shared, "To know you meant something to someone. To know I influenced someone to think twice. If you have a positive outlook on life you can help anyone." Echo stated, "Mentoring expands you. When you help someone to achieve a self-fulfilling goal, it gives you a feeling of success." Foxtrot shared, "When I see someone who I have mentored, to hear them say I was part of their success makes me feel so good. It's a feeling that cannot be replaced or explained." They emphasized that being able to touch someone's life in a way that may not have been possible before the mentoring experience makes them feel like they have given back to society. Golf shared, "The most worthwhile words to hear from someone you mentored are, 'You Changed My Life.'" Hearing those words makes her feel like she have accomplished something and helped someone. All respondents agreed that personal fulfillment is greater than any tangible reward, any day of the week.

Data Collection Analysis Procedures

Each interview was immediately transcribed after completion of the interview. This allowed the researcher to identify similarities in findings and categorize the information. After interviews and transcriptions were completed, data reduction, coding, and categorization were done and emergent themes arose (See Table 4).

To further analyze the data collected, the researcher made notes of key words and phrases and then generated a list of repetitive phrases and statements that each participant deemed vital (Table 2). From these statements emerging themes were developed and documented. These emerging themes were further analyzed to construct specific categories that involved similar thought patterns expressed by the research participants (Table 3). This process involved the connecting of relevant segments of data to form categories and clusters of information. In this study, the themes emerged provided specific descriptions of the lived mentoring experiences of the participants. The researcher applied the themes that emerged to this study as they adequately defined or answered the research questions. The themes that emerged are as follows: Same-Race Gender Mentoring, Mentoring and Acceptance, Mentoring and Career Advancement, and Giving Back by Mentoring Others.

Table 4. Themes

Question 1	Question 2	Question 3	Question 4	Question 5	Question 6
Organizational (formal – involuntary), identifiable experiences	Organizational requirements (formal)	If they don't want to be mentored	Mentor would try harder, different technique	Offers mentor professional growth, enhances leadership qualities	Personal fulfillment
Organizational (formal – involuntary)	Barriers that hinder success		Mentor would try harder, different technique	Offers mentor professional growth, enhances leadership qualities	Personal fulfillment
In need of help	Someone who wants help	If they don't want to be mentored		Offers mentor professional growth, enhances leadership qualities	Personal fulfillment

Table 4. Themes *continued*

Question 1	Question 2	Question 3	Question 4	Question 5	Question 6
Organizational (formal – involuntary)	Someone who wants help	Would never consider not mentoring	Mentor would try harder, different technique	Offers mentor professional growth	Personal fulfillment
	Someone who wants help	If they don't want to be mentored	Does not affect professional reputation	Offers mentor professional growth	Personal fulfillment
Identifiable experiences	Barriers that hinder success	Would never consider not mentoring		Offers mentor professional growth	Personal fulfillment
Organizational (formal – involuntary)	Barriers that hinder success	Would never consider not mentoring	Mentor would try harder, different Technique	Offers mentor professional growth	Personal fulfillment
In need of help	Someone who wants help		Does not affect professional reputation	Offers mentor professional growth	Personal fulfillment
In need of help	Someone who wants help	If they don't want to be mentored	Does not affect professional reputation	Offers mentor professional growth	Personal fulfillment
In need of help	Someone who wants help	Would never consider not mentoring	Does not affect professional reputation	Offers mentor professional growth	Personal fulfillment

Themes

The four (4) themes that emerged from the data collection in this study are: same-race mentoring, mentoring and gender, emotional support, and giving back by mentoring others.

Theme 1. Same-Race-Gender Mentoring

The previous literature suggested that African American women would be challenged to form strong mentoring relationships with protégés of the same race and gender. Kram (1985) identified that women are more reluctant to mentor due to time constraints, token status, and lack of self-confidence. The present study revealed that these same components found to hinder mentoring are the same barriers that would influence an African American woman to mentor. The women in this study were willing to give their time, were not concerned with what position they held, and displayed strong self confidence while interviewing. While Kram (1985) identified these components as challenges, the African American women interviewed for this present study revealed that these are barriers that encourage them to mentor. These women were able to empathize with these barriers because of identifiable experiences. Alpha shared, "When you identify with someone you tend to mentor them whether it's required or not. Many of us mentor everyday and on a regular basis because it's in our nature. I too had barriers at some point in time, but someone mentored me and helped aid in my success." Being able to identify with both sex and race is beneficial in a mentoring relationship. Where one race may consider the components mentioned above as barriers that would hinder someone from being chosen, another race would consider those barriers as a reason for the possible protégé to be selected because they can identify with those barriers. Bravo shared, "I grew up in an urban area and I prefer working with protégés that live in urban areas. They seem to have multiple barriers

68

present and benefit from being mentored. When I get a protégé who is defiant or tries to go against the grain, it makes me try harder to reach them because I was the same way and I can identify with what they're going through."

Theme 2. Mentoring and Acceptance

In reference to the protégé selection process, Allen (2003) indicated that motives for mentoring varied in relation to the importance of protégé ability and willingness to learn. Allen stated that mentors motivated by intrinsic reward are more likely to favor protégé willingness to learn as important in the protégé selection process. The present study confirmed Allen's (2003) findings. The present study revealed that African American women are motivated by intrinsic reward and protégé willingness to learn is an important component of the protégé selection process. Question 3 in this study offered information that this theme was derived from. Foxtrot shared, "When I see someone who I have mentored, to hear them say I was part of their success makes me feel so good. It's a feeling that cannot be replaced or explained."

Young and Perrewe (2000) revealed that mentors are more satisfied with a protégé who is open to advisement and coaching. The present study confirmed that African American women believe, if mentoring is to be effective, a protégé's openness to advisement and coaching is necessary. Echo shared, "You have a lot of protégés who don't see the potential you see in them. In cases like this the mentoring experience would be ineffective because the protégé is closed off from the start. You can only mentor individuals that want to be mentored." Protégé's openness to be coached or accept help was a reason given for not choosing to mentor. If a possible protégé is not willing to accept the help, African American women believe engaging in the mentoring relationship would prove ineffective.

69

Theme 3. Mentoring and Career Advancement

One risk associated with mentoring involves protégé performance. Ragins and Cotton (1993) stated that protégé performance is viewed as a reflection of the mentor's competency. The previous study suggests that having a low performing protégé would impact a mentor's reputation negatively. The present study revealed the opposite. Nine out of 10 African American women who participated in the present study did not feel being a mentor to a low performing protégé would have a negative effect on their career.

In contrast, the women in this study actually prefer low performing protégés. Delta shared, "I prefer the protégés that are hard to reach or inner-city protégés because I was an inner-city protégé. You have to practice what you preach with low performing protégés. Service is the key." Respondents suggested that low performing protégés improve their leadership skills and enhance professional growth. Low performing protégés influence them to come up with different ways to mentor and makes them try harder. When asked to explain further, Foxtrot shared, "Working with a low performing protégé helps my professionalism. It encourages me to come up with different ideas and ways to reach a protégé. It teaches me patience and also displays my leadership qualities with the company." The African American women in this study did not deem failure as an option. Hotel shared, "Mentoring gives real life experience that can be applied in the workplace." The participants in this study acknowledged that obstacles are presented so that new solutions can emerge.

Theme 4. Giving Back by Mentoring Others

The present study revealed that informal and formal mentoring networks are important components that contribute to personal and career growth. Responses to Question 6 in this study, is where this theme was derived. The African American women who participated in this study believe that giving back to others is more fulfilling than any tangible reward. The present study revealed that personal growth has a direct impact on career advancement. Golf shared, "Mentoring has a positive affect because I want to do this it's my passion and passion speaks for itself." African American women participate in mentoring relationships for intrinsic reward. Echo emphasized that, "Mentoring expands your personally, it's self-fulfilling, and gives a feeling of success." Career advancement is the after effect of these women doing something that comes natural to them and as a bonus.

Summary

Data analysis, data collection, demographics, emerging themes, and a re-introduction of the research questions were presented in Chapter 4. Each research question was presented separately and findings were discussed. Commonalities that emerged from the data were used to form themes. These four themes were; Same-Race-Gender Mentoring, Mentoring and Acceptance, Mentoring and Career Advancement, and Giving Back by Mentoring Others. Key findings of the data and limitations of the study will be discussed in Chapter 5. Based on these key findings, recommendations for future research studies will be provided.

CHAPTER 5. DISCUSSION, IMPLICATIONS, RECOMMENDATIONS

As mentioned earlier, previous mentoring research was conducted from the view of the mentor, and predominantly Caucasian mentors and protégés were the sample. Little is known about African American mentors and African American protégés that they mentor (Breakfield, 2010). Also, in addition to focusing on Caucasian mentors and protégés, past literature mainly focused on the view of the protégé. As such, the present study represents an attempt to examine mentoring relationships from the view of African American women mentors.

The present study examined the mentoring attitudes and preferences of African American women in Human Service leadership. The African American women, who participated in this study, are currently mentoring or have mentored. From the analysis presented in Chapter 4, Chapter 5 will present key findings of the study, followed by the limitations of the research. Based on the results, recommendations from the data are presented, and the study concludes with future research recommendations.

Review of the Research Problem and Purpose

As aforementioned, mentoring involves the mentor and the protégé combining responsibilities and roles to enhance a collaborative relationship. It has been suggested that a successful mentoring relationship is a vital component for career advancement and job satisfaction (Allen, 2007). If opportunities are not available, it could hinder career success for possible protégés and mentors. In previous studies, women were perceived to be more reluctant to mentor due to barriers. Previous studies also suggested that organizational success is a factor in willingness to mentor others (Allen, Poteet, Russell, & Dobbins, 1997). Women currently

72

hold the same positions as males and, oftentimes, earn the same salaries. However, this analogy does not pertain to African American women in Human Services.

Race and gender are holding African American women back in the leadership sector of Human Services (Combs, 2003). Combs' research has shown that workplace social networks involve socialization systems (like that of mentoring) which offer opportunities for career advancement. Literature is limited on mentoring among African American women and mentoring within Human Service organizations. The present study was done to further research in the Human Services field. The study examines the attitudes and preferences in mentoring among African American women in Human Service leadership.

Significance of the Study Findings

This study is significant because leadership is an important component that affects organizational performance (Straus et al., 2013). If opportunities are not available for African American women to be leaders in Human Services, it will be hard for them to produce future African American women leaders in Human Services. Mentoring involves a more experienced individual passing on knowledge and experience to a less experienced individual. This study examined mentoring relationships from the perspectives of African American female mentors within Human Services. The results of this study can be used to further research in the mentoring field and in the Human Services leadership field.

Analysis of the Research Process

The data collected during this study were organized into practical categories for the purpose of forming themes that coincide with the demographic questionnaire and the interview questions set forth for this study. During this process, textural descriptions, identification of probable meanings, construction of description of meanings, and personal experiences were factors that assisted in analyzing the data collected for this study. The research in this study was reflective of a purposeful sample that represented the phenomenon being studied.

Key Findings of the Study

The key findings for the present study confirmed that protégé willingness to learn is a main component in the protégé selection process. The current study also posits that participating in a mentoring relationship would have a positive effect on career advancement. Kram (1985) indicated that mentors are attracted to high performing protégés. In contrast, the present study indicated African American women prefer low performing protégés because it enhances their leadership qualities rather than affecting their reputation in a negative way. This study suggests that there is no component that would make African American women not want to mentor a protégé in need because of the personal fulfillment that is gained from helping others. In fact, during the interview Delta stated, "Mentoring a protégé is an internal reward that cannot be replaced."

Many other studies on mentoring have focused on formal mentoring programs within organizations (Kram, 1985; Allen, 2007; Allen & Poteet, 1999; Ragins, Cotton, & Miller, 2000). In contrast, the present study focused on formal and informal mentoring among African American women in Human Service leadership. Outside of formal mentoring programs, mentors have control over who they want to mentor. The focus of the current study on both types made it possible to examine what attracts mentors to their chosen protégés. Previous research has primarily been driven by two (2) theories: the similarity-attraction paradigm and social

74

exchange theory. The similarity-attraction paradigm suggests that mentors will be attracted to those they perceive to be similar to themselves (Byrne, 1971). Racial Identity Development theory, used by this study, posits this same truth and the present study also supports Byrne's findings. African American women suggest 'identifiable experiences' will enable the mentor to relate to the protégés in ways that someone from a different race could not.

Social Exchange theory suggests that individuals enter into relationships in which they believe the rewards will be greater than costs (Blau, 1964; Ragins & Scandura, 1999). Ragins and Scandura found individuals develop perceptions regarding costs and benefits associated with being a mentor. In contrast, the present study found that there is little to nothing that would prompt an African American female not to mentor. Cost and benefit is not a component that weighed heavy on the perceptions of mentoring for African American women. However, this study did find that African American women mentor for intrinsic reward and personal fulfillment. These components, on the other hand, could be considered a benefit that costs nothing.

Discussion of Key Findings in Relation to Literature in the Field

Successful mentoring relationships are a vital component for career advancement and job satisfaction (Allen, 2007). The current study confirmed Allen's findings and also shed light on the reasons African American women may not be advancing in the Human Services leadership field. If little or no opportunities are given for African American women to participate in the mentoring paradigm, their ability to advance in their careers will diminish and they will lack job satisfaction. Little research is currently available on mentoring among African American women in Human Services. This present study offers insight and understanding on the impact mentoring

75

relationships have on African American women organizational success in Human Services.

According to Bass (2010) African Americans need mentoring like they need oxygen. Bass posits mentorship helps one uncover the opportunities and possibilities that are beyond their grasp. Mentorship is a developmental relationship (Bass). African American women must openly celebrate each other while formulating healthy relationships and networks. Mentorship within Human Services will allow healthy relationships and networks to be formed.

Practical Implications

The practical findings of this study suggest that there are a low number of African American females in leadership positions in Human Service because of the scarce availability of mentoring opportunities. Like Allen (2007), the current study found that participating in mentoring relationships within an organization creates job satisfaction and allows opportunities for leadership qualities to be displayed. Thus, opportunities for promotion and advancement within an organization are directly related to mentoring opportunities. The themes that emerged from this study substantiate this claim. The themes that emerged from this study also suggest that it is because of being mentored that African American women feel a need to mentor. *Giving Back by Mentoring Others* was a theme that emerged that offers African American women a personal fulfillment that cannot be achieved through tangible rewards. It is safe to infer that unless mentoring opportunities are created for African American female leaders in Human Service to mentor other African American women, there will continue to be a deficiency of African American women in Human Service leadership.

If mentoring is made a part of one's job description it would promote employee's to mentor others on a regular basis. The organization that participated in the present study offers

76

mentoring as one of their core values. This opportunity is one reason the participants have been with this organization as long as they have. Mentoring within organization promotes healthy working relationships and offers a chance for individuals to display leadership qualities. These components lead to career advancement and job satisfaction.

Theoretical Implications

The theoretical framework for this study was Leader-Member Exchange theory (LMX) and Racial Identity Development theory. In comparison to mentoring, LMX focuses on the relationship between the superior and the subordinate. The leader provides support, consideration, and assistance. In contrast, LMX leaders are mandated by duty and will not go beyond these limits (Lunenburg, 2010). Mandated duty is where mentoring and LMX differ in context. The current study suggests that African American female mentors are willing to step outside the box to reach their protégés. African American female mentors are willing to go beyond their mandated duty to ensure they reach their protégé because they know the severity of not reaching them. Not reaching a possible protégé could negatively affect the protégés future and the protégé's ability to advance. By aligning LMX theory with mentoring, this study contributed to concepts of LMX theory. There was a gap in literature on LMX theory as it relates to mentoring and African American females. The results of this study aligned with concepts of LMX theory and examined LMX's influence on mentoring relationships among African American women in Human Service leadership.

Racial Identity Development theory focuses on the collective attributes of a groups that exists and identity of the group. These attributes include: beliefs, values, habits, lived experiences, and attitudes. Collaboratively, the African American women in this study proved that Racial Identity Development does have an impact on the how a particular group will view mentoring. This study indicates that African American female mentors prefer low performing protégés because it pushes them to be inventive, work harder, and step outside the box. In contrast, Allen's (2004) study found that low performing protégés was a component that would make a Caucasian male or female and African American male mentor not want to pick a protégé. It is safe to infer that the same things that would make other races not mentor prompt African American women to mentor. It is possible, however, that this finding could be due to the nurturing component that African American women may possess and be more multifaceted than simply gender and/or race related. Similarly, Allen suggested that protégé selection is likely based on a combination of demographic, motivational, and personality variables. This concept aligns with Racial Identity Development theory in that it focuses on the collective attributes of a group as well, and demonstrates support for the concepts of Racial Identity Development theory.

Limitations of the Study

The limitations of this study would have to be in direct reference to the small sample size used for this study. Creswell (1998) suggested that sample size for qualitative methodologies range from 5 to 25 participants and at least 6 to conduct an efficient study. Ten (10) was the targeted and acquired number of participants interviewed for this study with saturation achieved with this number. This limitation will not be addressed because it is common in qualitative studies. In qualitative studies, samples are small and said to not necessarily represent the broader population. Thus, it has been inferred that it is not known how far qualitative results can be generalized. Another limitation is in reference to the geographic area. There was only one 1 metropolitan geographic area used for this study due to cost and convenience. As a result, findings may not be generalizable outside of the urban United States Midwest.

Recommendations

Results from this study strongly suggest that African American women should seek the aid of a protégé to assist with career advancement and enhancement of job satisfaction. The present study sought to understand the attitudes and preferences of African American women. However, there are other minorities that would benefit from knowledge surrounding how mentoring could impact their careers so research should be expanded to all races. This study also focused only on the female population and would suggest that men may not face the same barriers as women. Statistics show that African American men hold more leadership positions than females and it may be easier for an African American male to find an identifiable protégé to mentor (and vice versa). The Human Services field would benefit from future studies involving a male population and other minority groups. A comparison study comprising African American men and women would assist with furthering mentoring literature in the Human Service leadership field by examining similarities and differences between the genders.

Conclusions

Based on the research conducted, the findings suggest that African American women do face an obstacle to organizational success in relation to mentoring opportunities. The participants who were interviewed were all protégés at one point and exclaimed that their success is due largely in part to the mentoring bestowed upon them. Now, their job satisfaction and career advancement is in direct relation to them being able to give back by mentoring others.

One of the themes that emerged from this study was 'Giving Back by Mentoring Others.' The African American women in this study felt an obligation to mentor others because of their past experiences as protégés. From this analogy, it is safe to infer that if African American women in leadership positions and entry level positions are not given the opportunity to mentor, it could lead to dissatisfaction on the job and impact their organizational success. Mentoring is a key component in organizational success that leads to job satisfaction and career advancement. Mentoring should be implemented in all Human Service organizations. Implementing mentoring relationships within Human Service organizations will promote healthy and effective organizational growth.

This study found that same-race-gender mentoring relationships are an important component of the mentoring paradigm because individuals that share the same morals and values will be able to share identifiable experiences. This is not to say that individuals of different genders and races cannot have effective mentoring relationships. However, same-race-gender mentoring relationships will be enhanced because of the mentor and protégé being able to identify with one another. To maximize an organization's return on investment for mentoring, formal mentoring programs should incorporate options for same-race-gender mentoring opportunities. This study supports that offering the same-race-gender component in mentoring will enhance or maximize the results gathered from mentoring. While mentoring is a helpful tool that promotes workplace comradery, it also increases career satisfaction for the individuals involved in the exchange (the protégé and the mentor). Increased career satisfaction will, sequentially, influence the protégé to become a mentor and the mentor to keep mentoring. It will also help promote the idea of giving individuals the opportunity to display leadership qualities which affect career advancement.

Mentoring is a very important component in the paradigm of organizational success. Mentoring is a career tool that increases benefits for the agency, the mentor, and the protégé.

The current study offers evidence that being able to participate in a identifiable experience with a mentor within an organizational realm can be the difference between career success and career failure. If more opportunities for African American women to mentor within Human Service organization are given, the resultant outcome will be increased job satisfaction and longevity, career advancement, and increased numbers of African American women in Human Service leadership positions.

References

Allen, T. D. (2003). Mentoring others: A dispositional and motivational approach. *Journal of Vocational Behavior, 62*, 134-154.

Allen, T. D. (2004). Protégé selection by mentors: Contributing individual and organizational factors. *Journal of Vocational Behavior, 65*, 469-483.

Allen, T. D. (2007). *Mentoring relationships from the perspective of the mentor. In B. R. Ragins & K. E. Kram (Eds). The handbook of mentoring at work: Theory, research and practice*, pp. 123-147. Thousand Oaks, CA: Sage.

Allen, T. D., Eby, L. T., & Lentz, E. (2006). The relationship between formal mentoring program characteristics and perceived program effectiveness. *Personnel Psychology, 59*, 125-153.

Allen, T. D., & Poteet, M. L. (1999). Developing effective mentoring relationships: Strategies from the mentor's viewpoint. *Career Development Quarterly, 48*, 59-73.

Allen, T. D., Poteet, M. L., & Burroughs, S. M. (1997). The mentor's perspective: A qualitative inquiry and future research agenda. *Journal of Vocational Behavior, 51*, 70-89.

Allen, T. D., Poteet, M. L., & Russell, J. E. A. (2000). Protégé selection by mentors: What makes the difference? *Journal of Organizational Behavior, 21*, 271-282.

Allen, T. D., Poteet, M. L., Russell, J. E. A., & Dobbins, G. H. (1997). A field study of factors related to supervisors' willingness to mentor others. *Journal of Vocational Behavior, 50*, 1-22.

American Public Human Services Association. (2013). On the road to a 21st century business model: Where are health and human services organizations today? Retrieved from http://www.nwi.aphsa.org.

Ary, D., Jacobs, L. C., & Razavieh, A. (1996). *Introduction to research in education*. Fort Worth, TX: Harcourt Brace College Publishers.

Assel, H., & Keon, J. (1982). Nonsampling vs. sampling errors in survey research. *Journal of Marketing, 46*(2), 114-123.

Bartlett, J. E., Kotrlik, J. W., & Higgins, C. C. (2001). Organizational research: Determining appropriate sample size in survey research. *Information Technology, Learning, and Performance Journal, 19*(1), 43-50.

Bass, K. T. (2010). Mentorship is as important as oxygen. *Black Enterprise: Wealth for Life.*

Baxter, P., & Jack, S. (2008). Qualitative case study methodology: Study design and implementation for novice researchers. *The Qualitative Review, 13*(4), 544-559.

Bell, E. L. (1990). The bicultural life experiences of career-oriented Black women: Summary. *Journal of Organizational Behavior, 11*(6), 459.

Bell, E. L., & Nkomo, S. (2001). *Our separate ways: Black and white women and the struggle for professional identity.* Boston, MA: Harvard Business Press.

Bernard, L. L. (1926). *An introduction to social psychology.* New York, NY: Holt.

Billett, S. (2003). Workplace mentors: Demands and benefits. *Journal of Workplace Learning, 15,* 105-113.

Blau, P. M. (1964). *Exchange and power in social life.* New York, NY: John Wiley and Sons.

Breakfield, F. A. (2010). Encircled by sisterhood: Mentoring experiences of African American women in Delta Sigma Theta. Retrieved from: http://digitalcommons.georgiasouthern.edu/cgi/viewcontent.cgi?article=1531&context=etd.

Brotherton, P. R. (1998). It's time for a career workout. *Black Enterprise, 28*(11), 82.

Bruce, M. A. (1995). Mentoring women doctoral students: What counselor educators and supervisors can do. *Counselor Education & Supervision, 35*(2), 139-149.

Cacioppe, R. 1997. Leadership moment by moment. *Leadership & Organization Development Journal, 18*(7), 335.

Caelli, K., & Mill, R. L. (2003). Clear as mud. *International Journal Qualitative Methods, 2*(2), 1-23.

Canary, D. J., & Dindia, K. (1998). *Sex differences and similar in communication: Critical essays and Empirical investigations of sex and gender in interaction.* New York, NY: Lawrence Erlbaum Associates.

Catalyst. (2004). *Advancing African American women in the workplace: What managers need to know.* Retrieved from http://www.catalyst.org/publication/20/advancing-african-american-women-in-the-workplace-what-managers-need-to-know.

Chen, C., Hickman, J. T., & Garcia, F. N. (2000). America's 50 best companies for minorities. *Fortune, 142*(2), 190-200.

Clawson, J. G., & Kram, K. E. (1984). Managing cross-gender mentoring. *Business Horizons, 2*(3), 22-32.

Collins, P. H. (2000). *Black feminist thought: Knowledge, consciousness, and the politics of empowerment*. New York, NY: Routledge.

Colvin, R. B., & Ashman, A. (2010). Roles, risks, and benefits of peer mentoring relationships in higher education. *Mentoring & Tutoring: Partnership in Learning, 18*(2), 121-134.

Combs, G. (2003). The duality of race and gender for managerial African American women: Implications of informal social networks on career advancement. Retrieved August 5, 2013 from http://digitalcommons.unl.edu/managementfacpub/31.

Conway, C. (2002). Leadership skills approach. *Ivey Management Services, 3*, 81-83.

Cooper, S., & Endacott, R. (2007). Generic qualitative research: A design for qualitative research in emergency care. *Emergency Medical Journal, 24*, 816-819.

Cooper, D., & Schindler, P. (2008). *Business research methods*. New York, NY: Jossey-Bass.

Corbin, J., & Strauss, A. (1990). Grounded theory research: Procedures, canons, and evaluative criteria. *Qualitative Sociology, 13*, 3-21.

Cox, T., & Nkomo, S. M. (1986). Differential performance appraisal criteria: A field study of Black and White managers. *Group and Organizational Studies, 11*(1/2), 101-119.

Crawford, K., & Smith, D. (2005). The we and the us: Mentoring African American women. *Journal of Black Studies, 36*(1), 52-67.

Creswell, J. W. (2009). *Research design: Qualitative, quantitative, and mixed methods approaches* (3rd ed.). Los Angeles, CA: Sage.

Creswell, J. W. (1998). *Qualitative inquiry and research design. Choosing among five traditions*. Thousand Oaks, CA: Sage.

Cross, W. E. (1971). The negro to black conversion experience. *Black World, 20*, 13-27.

Cross, W. E. (1991). *Shades of black: Diversity in African American identity*. Philadelphia, PA: Temple University Press.

Dansereau, F., Graen, G., & Haga, W. J. (1975). A vertical dyad linkage approach to leadership within formal organizations: A longitudinal investigation of the role-making process. *Organizational Behavior and Human Performance, 13*, 46-78.

Davidson, M. N., & Foster-Johnson, L. (2001). Mentoring in preparation of graduate researchers of color. *Review of Educational Research, 71*(4), 549-574.

Davis, K. S. (2001). Peripheral and subversive: Women making connections and challenging the boundaries of the science community. *Science Education, 85*, 368-409.

Denzin, N. K., & Lincoln, Y. S. (2000). *Handbook of qualitative research*. London, EN: Sage.

Dreher, G. F., & Ash, R. A. (1990). A comparative study of mentoring among men and women in managerial, professional, and technical positions. *Journal of Applied Psychology, 75*(5), 539-546.

Dreher, G. F., & Cox, T. H. (1996). Race, gender, and opportunity: A study of compensation attainment and the establishment of mentoring relationships. *Journal of Applied Psychology, 75*(5), 539-546.

DuBois, D. L., Holloway, B. E., Valentine, J. C., & Cooper, H. (2002). Effectiveness of mentoring programs: A meta-analytical review. *American Journal of Community Psychology, 30*, 157–197.

Eby, L., Rhodes, J., & Allen, T. (2007). Definition and evolution of mentoring. Malden, MA; Blackwell Publishing.

Emerson, R. M. (1976). Social exchange theory. *Annual Review of Sociology, 2*, 335-362.

Friedman, R., Kane, M., & Cornfield, D. B. (1998). Social support and career optimism: Examining the effectiveness of network groups among black managers. *Human Relations, 51*(9), 1155-1177.

Gibbs, G. (2007). *Analyzing qualitative data*. London, EN: Sage.

Gill, R. (2006). *Theory and practice of leadership*. Thousand Oaks, CA: Sage.

Glaser, B. & Strauss, A. (1967). *The discovery of grounded theory: Strategies for qualitative research*. New York, NY: Aldine Publishing Company.

Graen, G. B., & Uhl-Bien, M. (1995). Relationship-based approach to leadership: Development of leader-member exchange (LMX) theory of leadership over 25 years: Applying a multi-level multi-domain perspective. *Leadership Quarterly, 6*, 219-247.

Green, S. G., & Bauer, T. N. (1995). Supervisory mentoring by advisors: Relationships with doctoral student potential, productivity, and commitment. *Personnel Psychology, 48*, 537-561.

Grieco, E. M., & Cassidy, R. C. (2001). *Overview of race and Hispanic origin*. Washington, DC: U.S. Department of Commerce, Economics and Statistics Administration and U.S. Census Bureau.

Grossman, J. B., & Rhodes, J. E. (2002). The test of time: Predictors and effects of duration in youth mentoring. *American Journal of Community Psychology, 30,* 199-219.

Hansman, C. A. (2002). *Mentoring: From Athena to the 21st century*. Denver, CO: ERIC Publications.

Healy, M., & Perry, C. (2000). Comprehensive criteria to judge validity and reliability of qualitative research within the realism paradigm. *Qualitative Market Research-An International Journal, 3*(3), 118-126.

Heilbrunn, J. (1994). Can leadership be studied? *The Wilson Quarterly, 18*(2), 65-73.

Helms, J. E. (1990). *Black and white racial identity: Theory, research, and practice*. New York, NY: Greenwood Press.

Helms, J. E. (1994). The *conceptualization of racial identity and other racial constructs*. San Francisco, CA: Jossey-Bass.

Helms, J. E. (1996). *Toward a methodology for measuring and assessing racial identity as distinguished from ethnic identity*. Lincoln, NE: Buros Institute of Mental Measurement.

Helms, J. E. (1997). Race is not ethnicity. *American Psychologist, 52*, 1246-1247.

Hewstone, M., Hantzi, A., & Johnston, L. (1991). Social categorization and person memory: The pervasiveness of race as an organizing principle. *European Journal of Social Psychology, 21*, 517-528.

Homans, C. G. (1950). *The human group*. New York, NY: Harcourt, Brace & World.

Homans, C. G. (1961). *Social behavior: Its elementary forms*. New York, NY: Harcourt, Brace & World.

Horner, M. (1997). Leadership theory: Past, present and future. *Team Performance Management, 3*(4), 270.

Human Services Summit. (2010). The next generation of human services: Realizing the vision. *Leadership for a Networked World*.

Hunt, D., & Michael, C. (1983). Mentorship: A career training and development tool. *Academy of Management Review, 8*(3), 475-485.

King, J. & Gomez, G. (2007). *The American college president: 2007 edition*. Washington, DC: American Council on Education Center for Policy Analysis.

Kanter, R. M. (1977). *Men and women of the corporation*. New York, NY: Basic Books.

Kram, K. E. (1985). *Mentoring at work*. Glenview, IL: Scott, Foresman.

Kram, K. E., & Hall, D. T. (1996). Mentoring in a context of diversity and turbulence. In E. E. Kossek & S. Lobel (Eds.). *Managing diversity: Human resources strategies for transforming the work place* (pp. 108-136). Cambridge, MA: Blackwell.

Kram, K. E., & Isabella, L. A. (1985). Mentoring alternatives: The role of peer relationships in career development. *Academy of Management, 28*(1), 110-132.

Kvale, S., & Brinkmann, S. (2009). *Interviews: Learining the craft of qualitative research interviewing.* Los Angeles, CA: Sage.

Levinson, D. J., Darrow, C. N., Klein, E. B., & Levinson, M. (1978). *Seasons of a man's life.* New York, NY: Random House.

Lewis, J., Packard, T., & Lewis, M. (2007). *Management of human service programs* (4th ed.). Belmont, CA: Thompson/Brooks Cole.

Lincoln, Y. S., & Guba, E. G. (1985). *Naturalistic inquiry.* Beverly Hills, CA: Sage.

Lomax, R. G. (2007). *An introduction to statistical concepts* (2nd ed.). Mahwah, NJ: Erlbaum.

Lunenburg, F. C. (2010). Leader-Member Exchange Theory: Another perspective on the leadership process. *International Journal of Management, Business, and Administration, 13*(1).

Mason, M. (2010). Sample size and saturation in PhD studies using qualitative interviews. *Forum: Qualitative Social Research, 11*(3).

McNeece, C., & Thyer, B. (2004). Evidence-based practice and social work. *Journal of Evidence-Based Practice, 1*(1), 7-25.

Miles, M. B, & Huberman, M. A. (1994). *Qualitative data analysis: An expanded sourcebook.* Thousand Oaks, CA: Sage.

Newby, T. J., & Heide, A. (1992). The value of mentoring. *Performance Improvement Quarterly, 5*(4), 2-15.

Newhouse, R. P., Dearholt, S., Poe, S., Pugh, L. C., & White, K. M. (2007). Organizational change strategies for evidence-based practice. *Journal of Nursing Administration, 37*(12), 552-557.

Niehoff, B. P. (2006). Personality predictors of participation as a mentor. *Career Development International, 11*(4), 321-333.

Noe, R. A. (1988). Women and mentoring: A review and research agenda. *Academy of Management Review, 13*, 65-78.

Northouse, P. (2004). *Leadership: Theory and practice* (3rd ed.). Thousand Oaks, CA: Sage.

Offutt, P. K. (2011). *Mentoring among African American women: A quantitative study.* Ann Arbor, MI: UMI Dissertation Publishing.

Olson, K. (2006). Survey participation, nonresponse bias, measurement error bias, and total bias. *Public Opinion Quarterly, 70*(5), 737-758.

Ortiz-Walters, R., & Gilson, L. L. (2005). Mentoring in academia: An examination of the experiences of protégés of color. *Journal of Vocational Behavior, 67*, 459-475.

Packard, T. (2004). Leadership and performance in Human Services organizations. *Managing for Performance,* 143-164.

Peers, I. (1996). *Statistical analysis for education and psychology researchers.* Bristol, PA: Falmer Press.

Phinney, J. S. (1992). The multigroup ethnic identity measure: A new scale for use with diverse groups. *Journal of Adolescence Research, 7,* 156-176.

Pulukos, E. D. (2012). *Performance management: A roadmap for developing, implementing and evaluating performance management systems.* Alexandria, VA: SHRM Foundation.

Ragins, B. R. (1997). Diversified mentoring relationships in organizations: A power perspective. *Academy of Management Review, 22*(2), 482-521.

Ragins, B. R., & Cotton, J. L. (1999). Mentor functions and outcomes: A comparison of men and women in formal and informal mentoring relationships. *Journal of Applied Psychology, 84,* 529-550.

Ragins, B. R., & Cotton, J. L. (1993). Gender and willingness to mentor in organizations. *Journal of Management, 19,* 97-111.

Ragins, B. R., Cotton, J. L., & Miller, J. S. (2000). Marginal mentoring: The effects of type of mentor, quality of relationship, and program design on work and career attitudes. *Academy of Management Journal, 43,* 1177-1194.

Ragins, B. R., & Scandura, T. A. (1999). Burden or blessing? Expected costs and benefits of being a mentor. *Journal of Organizational Behavior, 20,* 493-509.

Ragins, B. R., & Verbos, A. K. (2007). *Positive relationships in action: Relational mentoring and mentoring schemas in the workplace.* Mahwah, NJ: Lawrence Erlbaum.

Rhodes, J., Lowe, S. R., Litchfield, L., & Walsh-Samp, K. (2008). The role gender in youth mentoring relationship formation and duration. *Journal of Vocational Behavior, 72,* 183-192.

Ritchie, J., Lewis, J. & Elam, G. (2003). *Designing and selecting samples. Qualitative research practice: A guide for social science students and researchers.* Thousand Oaks, CA: Sage.

Scandura, T. A. (1992). Mentorship and career mobility: An empirical investigation. *Journal of Organizational Behavior, 13*, 169-174.

Scandura, T. A., & Schriesheim, C. A. (1994). Leader-member exchange and supervisor mentoring as complementary constructs in leadership research. *Academy of Management Journal, 37*(6), 1588.

Schriesheim, C. A., Castro, S. L., & Cogliser, C. C. (1999). Leader-member exchange (LMX) research: A comprehensive review of theory, measurement, and data-analytic practices. *Leadership Quarterly, 10*(1), 63-113.

Sheared, V. (1994). *Giving voice: An inclusive model of instruction. A woman's perspective.* San Francisco, CA: Jossey-Bass.

Solomon, E. E., Bishop, R. C., & Bresser, R. K. (1986). Organization moderators of gender differences in career development: A facet classification. *Journal of Vocational Behavior, 29*, 27-41.

Stake, R. E. (1995). *The art of case study research.* Thousand Oaks, CA: Sage.

Stogdill, R. M. (1974). *Handbook of leadership: A survey of theory and research.* New York, NY: Free Press.

Stolte, J. F., Fine, G. A., & Cook, K. S. (2001). Sociological miniaturism: Seeing the big through the small in Social Psychology. *Annual Review of Sociology, 27*, 387-413.

Straus, S. E., Johnson, M. O., Marquez, C., & Feldman, M. D. (2013). Characteristics of successful and failed mentoring relationships: A qualitative study across two academic health careers. *Journal of Academic Medicine, 88*(1), 82-89.

Taylor, S. J., & Bogdan, R. (1998). *Introduction to qualitative research methods.* Hoboken, NJ: Wiley and Sons.

Thompson, C. E., & Carter, R. T. (1997). *Racial Identity Theory: Applications to individual, group, and organizational interventions.* Mahwah, NJ: Lawrence Erlbaum Associates.

Thorndike, E. (1932). *The fundamentals of learning.* Brooklyn, NY: AMS Press Inc.

Thurston, N. E., & King, K. M. (2004). Implementing evidence-based practice: Walking the talk. *Applied Nursing Research, 17*(4), 239-247.

Tonidaniel, S., Avery, D. R., & Phillips, M. G. (2007). Maximizing returns on mentoring: Factors affecting subsequent protégé performance. *Journal of Organizational Behavior, 28*, 89-100.

Trochim, W. M. (2000). The research methods knowledge base. Retrieved August 24, 2013, from http://www.socialresearchmethods.net/kb/.

Truckenbrodt, Y. B. (2000). The relationship between leader-member exchange and commitment and organizational citizenship behavior. *Acquisition Review Quarterly,* 233-242.

United States Census Bureau. (2007). U. S. census bureau: States & County Quickfacts. Retrieved August 5, 2013, from http://quickfacts.census.gov/qfd/states/00000.html.

Van Wart, M. (2003). Public sector leadership theory: An assessment. *Public Administration Review, 63*(2), 214-229.

Yin, R. K. (2003). *Case study research: Design and methods* (3rd ed.). Thousand Oaks, CA: Sage.

Young, A. M., & Perrewe, P. L. (2000). What did you expect: An examination of career related support and social support among mentors and protégés. *Journal of Management, 26,* 611-632.

Yukl, G. (1989). *Leadership in organizations.* Englewood Cliffs, NJ: Prentice Hall.

Zafirovski, M. (2005). Social exchange theory under scrutiny: A positive critique of its economic-behaviorist formulations. *Journal of Sociology,* 1-40.

Zenger, J., & Folkman, J. (2002). *The extraordinary leader.* New York, NY: McGraw-Hill.

APPENDIX B. DEMOGRAPHIC SURVEY

By: Tiffany Manning

1. Age

2. Highest level of education completed

3. Length of time in current position

4. Length of time in current organization

5. Type of industry

6. How long have you been a mentor?

APPENDIX C. INTERVIEW QUESTIONS

By: Tiffany Manning

1. Explain your process for selecting a protégé?

2. What components or qualities does a protégé need to possess to be selected?

3. What are some things that would make you consider not mentoring a possible protégé?

4. How does being a mentor to a low performing protégé affect your professional reputation?

5. Explain the affect mentoring, if any, has on career advancement?

6. What type of reward or fulfillment is achieved from being a mentor?

Made in the USA
Charleston, SC
10 January 2015